Sure Signs a Movie Character Is Doomed & Other Surprising Movie Lists

ALSO BY RICHARD ROEPER

He Rents, She Rents (with Laurie Viera)

Urban Legends

Hollywood Urban Legends

RICHARD ROEPER

**10
Sure Signs a Movie
Character Is Doomed
& Other Surprising
Movie Lists**

HYPERION   NEW YORK

Library of Congress Cataloging-in-Publication Data

Roeper, Richard
    Ten sure signs a movie character is doomed, and other surprising movie lists / Richard Roeper.—1st ed.
      p. cm.
    ISBN: 0-7868-8830-X
    1. Motion pictures—Miscellanea. I. Title.

   PN1998.R568   2003
   791.43'02'907—dc21

                                                    2002032831

Hyperion books are available for special promotions and premiums. For details contact Hyperion Special Markets, 77 West 66th Street, 11th floor, New York, New York 10023-6298, or call 212-456-0133.

Book design by Lorelle Graffeo

FIRST EDITION

10 9 8 7 6 5 4 3 2 1

Acknowledgments

"It's my privilege. Thank you."

With those five words in 1990, Joe Pesci (*GoodFellas*) gave the shortest and one of the best Academy Award speeches of all time. I'm going to have to go a little longer than that with my list of thank-yous, but I'll try to keep it brief, because the only people who read the Acknowledgments page are people looking for their names.

If you're not here and you expected to be here, it was a computer glitch. Honest.

Thanks to Robert and Margaret Roeper; Lynn and Nick Zona; Bob and Colleen Roeper; Laura Roeper; Sam Saunders; Laura Renee LeQuesne; John LeQuesne; Emily Roeper; Caroline Roeper; and Bobby Roeper. Family comes first.

Thanks also to: Bill Adee, Grace Adee, Leslie Baldacci, Bruce

Billmeyer, Susan Carlson, Jacqueline Carroll, Michelle Carney, Jennifer Ciminillo, Stuart Cleland, Jacqueline Colbert, Michael Cooke, John Cruickshank, Darcie Divita, Don Dupree, Roger Ebert, Laura Emerick, Robert Feder, Will Freeman, Wendy George, Andrea Gronvall, Drew Hayes, Susanna Homan, Mary Kellogg, David Kodeski, Rick Kogan, Janet LaMonica, Todd Musburger, Lia Papadopoulos, Phil Rosenthal, Bob Sirott, Nancy Stanley, Neil Steinberg, Barbara Warren, Jenniffer Weigel, Joyce Winnecke, Paige and Jim Wiser, Bill Zehme, and Bill Zwecker.

Thanks always to my agent, Sheree Bykofsky. She knows when to hold 'em and never folds 'em. Thanks to everyone at Hyperion, notably Jennifer Lang, and to my editors at the *Chicago Sun-Times* and the New York Times Syndicate.

Special kudos to David Plummer, whose research assistance on this book was invaluable.

And sincere thanks to the hundreds upon hundreds of *Ebert & Roeper* viewers who have written or called over the last three years to vent, to rant, to rave, or to ask me where I got my glasses. We don't always agree—but we always share a common love for the movies.

Introduction

In the summer of '92, hundreds of entertainment journalists from the United States, Great Britain, Brazil, Switzerland, Korea, Japan, Germany, Italy, and elsewhere swooped into Chicago for a weekend junket promoting *Batman Returns*, the most highly anticipated movie of the year. In addition to round-trip airfare, the junketeers were treated to an all-expenses-paid weekend at the luxurious Four Seasons Hotel just off Chicago's Magnificent Mile and were given treats that included a T-shirt, a travel bag, and a *Batman Returns* denim jacket. Their only journalistic obligation was to screen the film and to participate in and write about a series of press conference–type interviews with director Tim Burton and stars Michael Keaton, Michelle Pfeiffer, and Danny DeVito—who was in Chicago shooting *Hoffa* at the time, which is why the junket was taking place there rather than in

Hollywood, where such studio-funded love-fests occur nearly every weekend.

You've seen these events spoofed as schmoozy, smarmy affairs in films such as *Notting Hill* and *America's Sweethearts,* but junkets are such ridiculous spectacles in the first place that they're nearly impossible to satirize. What we really need is a documentary about the process—but the day a major studio allows a filmmaker to have carte blanche at a junket is the day Lorne Michaels receives the Irving Thalberg Award for making all those "Saturday Night Live" movies. This is why I cherish the memory of the Michael Keaton Q-and-A at the *Batman Returns* junket, at which the first and best of the Batmans punctured the pretentious attitude of the room by interrupting a long-winded and far too serious questioner by saying, and I quote:

"You know what? It's just a f------ movie. You know, there are movies, and then there's life. I think we're taking movies way too f------ seriously here."

God bless you, Michael Keaton. And by the way, you should have been nominated for Academy Awards for Best Actor *and* Best Supporting Actor for your roles in *Multiplicity*.

Don't get me wrong. I love movies. Movies are dreams set to music, and every time the lights drop and the curtains open and the projector starts to whir, I am filled with a sense of anticipation and excitement. Maybe THIS movie, this particular waking dream, will permeate my consciousness and sing to my soul and resonate with me forever, just as films like *The Maltese Falcon* and *The Last Picture Show* and *McCabe & Mrs. Miller* and *Pulp Fiction* and *Memento* and so many others have done in the past. Maybe this film will make my Top 10 list and become a must-own DVD and will be discussed with great passion by my friends and family.

Maybe this movie will make a difference.

Then again, maybe this movie will be *The Mummy's Back and There's Nothing You Can Do About It*, in which case I'd rather stick my head in a pot of boiling water than watch it more than once.

The best part about my job is I get to see just about every movie made. The worst part of my job is I HAVE to see just about every movie ever made. Though I'll never disagree with those who tell me I've got the greatest job in the world, the people who are saying that to me didn't have to see *The*

Sweetest Thing, *Clockstoppers*, *Death to Smoochy*, *Big Trouble*, and *National Lampoon's Van Wilder* in rapid succession.

This book was fueled by my lifelong love affair with good movies—and my resentment for the crap that's shoveled into theaters on a weekly basis. I will celebrate crisp writing, stellar acting, and inspired filmmaking in such lists as my favorite monologues of the last 25 years and the best sequels of all time, but I'm also going to release my venom on the worst Irish accents in cinematic history and the actors who have done nude scenes despite our most fervent wishes that they keep it on, keep it all on. I'm also shining the spotlight on movie clichés that have been done to death, and I'm going to poke some light fun at the likes of Michael Douglas and Ben Affleck. (They're living charmed lives. They can handle it.) If you're looking for a book of movie lists that tells you the real names of Cary Grant and John Wayne, this isn't it. But if you'd like to see the definitive list of movies in which Ben Affleck cries like a big fat baby, proceed directly to the register with this book in hand.

After all, I'm dedicating this book to you—the person who loves great films—but also loves hating bad movies.

Richard Roeper
August 2002

14 movies featuring Jay Leno interviewing or doing a monologue joke about the characters

14 movies featuring Jay Leno interviewing or doing a monologue joke about the characters

John Q. (2002)

Juwanna Mann (2002)

Space Cowboys (2000)

EDtv (1999)

Wag the Dog (1997)

Mad City (1997)

In & Out (1997)

Contact (1997)

Meet Wally Sparks (1997)

The Birdcage (1996)

The Flintstones (1994)

Major League II (1994)

Wayne's World 2 (1993)

Dave (1993)

actresses
who **still**
looked
great
even when
they were
disguised
as **men**

actresses who still looked great even when they were disguised as men

Julie Andrews in *Victor/Victoria* (1982)

Joyce Hyser in *Just One of the Guys* (1985)

Mira Sorvino in *Triumph of Love* (2001)

Gwyneth Paltrow in *Shakespeare in Love* (1998)

Hilary Swank in *Boys Don't Cry* (1999)

Zhang Ziyi in *Crouching Tiger, Hidden Dragon* (2000)

actresses
who have
yet
to do a
nude scene

actresses who have yet to do a nude scene

ody doubles don't count.

Anne Archer

Tyra Banks

Sandra Bullock

Nikki Cox

Kirsten Dunst

Sarah Michelle Gellar

Jennifer Love Hewitt

Janet Jackson

Beyoncé Knowles

Cheryl Ladd

Téa Leoni

Julia Louis-Dreyfus

Andie MacDowell

Julia Roberts

Winona Ryder

Brooke Shields

Jessica Simpson

Britney Spears

Barbra Streisand

Kristy Swanson

Raquel Welch

Zhang Ziyi

12 actors and actresses who took their clothes off when they should have kept them on

12 actors and actresses who took their clothes off when they should have kept them on

If you're young and beautiful and in great shape—like Denise Richards in *Wild Things* or Phoebe Cates when she stepped out of the pool in *Fast Times at Ridgemont High* or Penélope Cruz in just about every film she's done to date—there's no big risk in doing a nude scene. Especially if it's "integral to the part" and isn't "gratuitous," which is what every actor always says about doing nude scenes. (Funny how certain actresses, from Audrey Hepburn and Grace Kelly to Elizabeth Taylor to Julia Roberts and Michelle Pfeiffer, managed to avoid explicit nudity yet become international sex symbols anyway.)

I'm much more impressed—and, quite frankly, occasionally horrified—when a thespian who's not exactly buff does a nude scene. Herewith some talented and lovely but physically imperfect actors and actresses who have doffed their duds in the name of artistic expression:

Kathy Bates, *At Play in the Fields of the Lord* (1991)

Tyne Daly, *The Adultress* (1973)

Michael Douglas, *Basic Instinct* (1992)

Shelley Duvall, *Thieves Like Us* (1974)

Harvey Keitel, *Bad Lieutenant* (1992)

Sally Kirkland, *Amnesia* (1997) Kirkland was 53. Her implants were about 10. They were also about a 36DD.

k.d. lang, *Salmonberries* (1991)

Camryn Manheim, *The Road to Wellville* (1994)

Helen Mirren, *The Passion of Ayn Rand* (1999)

Geoffrey Rush, *Quills* (2000)

Jessica Tandy, *Camilla* (1994) Ms. Tandy was a beautiful young woman, but she was 85 when she went skinny-dipping in this film. And unless you're 96, an 85-year-old just doesn't look that great naked.

Aida Turturro, *Illuminata* (1998)

The **worst best movies of all time**

the worst best movies of all time

Seeing as how this is a book of lists, it might not seem fair for me to chide the American Film Institute (AFI) for its lists of the 100 greatest, funniest, most thrilling, etc., movies of all time—but I'll do it anyway. In this list-crazy world, the AFI rankings are taken seriously because the films are selected by a panel of respected journalists, directors, writers, actors, editors, cinematographers, critics, and historians—but every time they release one of these lists, some of the entries are, well, WRONG. From the 1998 AFI list of the 100 Greatest American Movies, 10 films that don't belong:

AFI #7: *The Graduate* (1967)

Mike Nichols's cynical attempt to define a generation was released in 1967, but there's no mention of Vietnam, the civil rights movement, political unrest, activism on college campuses, the Beatles, the Rolling Stones, drugs, or hippies. It's as if Benjamin's world has time-warped a decade, back to the late 1950s. With groundbreaking performances from Dustin Hoffman and Anne Bancroft and that unforgettable soundtrack from Simon and Garfunkel, The Graduate *certainly isn't a bad movie; it's just not a great one.*

AFI #36: *Midnight Cowboy* (1969)

Nothing against Dustin Hoffman, who would definitely make my list of the 100 greatest American actors, but once again he's in a movie that was hailed as a work of daring genius at the time, but has not held up. Hoffman and Jon Voight are strong, but the story is contrived, hokey, and flat.

AFI #41: *West Side Story* (1961)

There are some memorable songs, and the choreography is crisp—but if they were updating this list, Moulin Rouge! (2001) would get my vote to replace West Side Story, *with its ethnically incorrect casting, its dubbed vocals, and the quaint gang-rivalry-by-way-of-Shakespeare storyline.*

AFI #59: *Rebel Without a Cause* (1955)

Of James Dean's three theatrical films, this is the third best, renowned more for its star-crossed cast and its great title than the film itself. Watch it again and you'll be struck by the over-the-top performances from just about everybody, including Dean.

AFI #60: *Raiders of the Lost Ark* (1981)

Sure, this is a fun adventure story in the tradition of the Saturday matinee serials—but is it really the sixtieth best American movie ever made? For that matter, is it even the six hundredth best American movie ever made?

AFI #71: *Forrest Gump* (1994)

A huge hit with an Oscar-winning performance by Tom Hanks, but I think he showed more depth in Cast Away.

AFI #72: *Ben-Hur* (1959)

The special effects were impressive for their time, but the acting is laughable and the story drags on forever. Another film that's on the list more for its reputation than its artistic merits.

the worst best movies of all time

AFI #91: *My Fair Lady* (1964)

A perfectly adequate, mainstream, big-screen adaptation of a hit Broadway musical. And that's all it is.

AFI #99: *Guess Who's Coming to Dinner* (1967)

Preachy attempt to be socially significant hedges its bets. Sure, it was shocking at the time for a young white woman to bring home a black man—but the black man in question is Sidney Poitier, as a doctor, no less. It's not as if the girl came home and said, "Mom, Dad, I'd like you to meet Huey Newton. Huey, this is my mom and pop!"

AFI #100: *Yankee Doodle Dandy* (1942)

Another entertaining musical that has no business being ranked among the greatest 100 movies of all time.

10 movies that didn't make the AFI list but should have

10 movies that didn't make the AFI list but should have

His Girl Friday (1940)

Sullivan's Travels (1942)

The Quiet Man (1952)

Touch of Evil (1958)

McCabe & Mrs. Miller (1971)

Nashville (1975)

All the President's Men (1976)

National Lampoon's Animal House (1978)

Do the Right Thing (1989)

Reservoir Dogs (1992)

6 movies

that have **been released** since the **AFI list but** could be **considered** among the **100 greatest** of all time

6 movies that have been released since the AFI list but could be considered among the 100 greatest of all time

Saving Private Ryan (1998)

American Beauty (1999)

Traffic (2000)

A Beautiful Mind (2001)

Memento (2000)

Minority Report (2002)

II movies

that employed **James Brown's** "(I Got You) I Feel Good" to indicate that a character feels **good!**

11 movies that employed James Brown's "(I Got You) I Feel Good" to indicate that a character feels good!

Exit Wounds (2001)

Good Morning, Vietnam (1987)

Isn't She Great (2000)

Juwanna Mann (2002)

K-9 (1989)

Mr. Jones—as sung by Richard Gere (1993)

Mrs. Doubtfire (1993)

The Nutty Professor (1996)

Showtime (2002)

A Smile Like Yours (1997)

White Men Can't Jump (1992)

pop songs in permanent rotation on the movie soundtrack jukebox

pop songs in permanent rotation on the movie soundtrack jukebox

✓ **"All Star," by Smash Mouth**

> *Inspector Gadget* (1999)
>
> *Mystery Men* (1999)
>
> *Rat Race* (2001)
>
> *Shrek* (2001)

✓ **"Born to Be Wild," by Steppenwolf**

> *Born to Be Wild* (1995)—song performed by Green Jelly
>
> *Easy Rider* (1969)
>
> *Lost in America* (1985)
>
> *Recess: School's Out* (2001)

✓ **"Bad to the Bone," by George Thorogood & The Destroyers**

> *3000 Miles to Graceland* (2001)
>
> *Christine* (1983)
>
> *Terminator 2: Judgment Day* (1991)

✓ **"I Can See Clearly Now," by Johnny Nash**

> *Antz* (1998)—song performed by Neil Finn
>
> *Cool Runnings* (1993)—song performed by Jimmy Cliff
>
> *Deep Blue Sea* (1999)—song performed by Chantel Jones

Grosse Pointe Blank (1997)

Thelma & Louise (1991)

"I Will Survive," by Gloria Gaynor

Beyond Silence (1996)

Coyote Ugly (2000)—song performed by Sybersound

Dr. Dolittle 2 (2001)

First Wives Club (1996)

Four Weddings and a Funeral (1994)

In & Out (1997)

Man on the Moon (1999)—song performed by Tony Cliffton

The Adventures of Priscilla, Queen of the Desert (1994)

The Replacements (2000)

"Magic Carpet Ride," by Steppenwolf

Austin Powers: The Spy Who Shagged Me (1999)

Go (1999)

The Limey (1999)

Never Been Kissed (1999)

Outside Providence (1999)

"The Power," by Snap!

Coyote Ugly (2000)

Dr. Dolittle 2 (2001)

Hudson Hawk (1991)

Three Kings (1999)

Under Siege (1992)

pop songs in permanent rotation on the movie sound-track jukebox

√ **"Rock and Roll Part 2," by Gary Glitter**

Any Given Sunday (1999)

Bedazzled (2000)

D2: The Mighty Ducks (1994)

Duets (2000)

The Full Monty (1997)

Like Mike (2002)

Michael Jordan to the Max (2000)

The Replacements (2000)

Small Soldiers (1998)

Sugar & Spice (2001)

√ **"Spirit in the Sky," by Norman Greenbaum**

Angel Baby (1995)

Apollo 13 (1995)

Contact (1997)

The Fan (1996)

Household Saints (1993)

Maid to Order (1987)

Miami Blues (1990)

My Name Is Joe (1998)

Remember the Titans (2000)

Saving Grace (2000)

A Simple Plan (1998)

Superstar (1999)

The War (1994)

Wayne's World 2 (1993)

✓ "Takin' Care of Business," by Bachman-Turner Overdrive

Highway 61 (1991)

A Knight's Tale (2001)

Last Night (1998)

The Replacements (2000)

"Walking on Sunshine," by Katrina and the Waves

American Psycho (2000)

High Fidelity (2000)

Look Who's Talking (1989)

The Master of Disguise (2002)

The Secret of My Succe$s (1987)

when
singers
try to
act

when singers try to act

from Al Jolson to Elvis to Barbra Streisand to Britney Spears, popular singers have made the transition to the big screen— sometimes as musical stars, occasionally as serious actors. Some, like Bing Crosby, Frank Sinatra, and Cher, have won Academy Awards; others, such as Dwight Yoakam and Tom Waits, have carved out nice second careers as reliable character actors. And others are so amateurish they wouldn't get cast on a soap opera if they didn't have pop chart success on their résumés. Hello, Lance Bass and Britney Spears!

Some of the best and most successful singer/actors, along with a few of their notable cinematic contributions, in musicals as well as straight dramatic and/or comedic roles:

The Beatles—*A Hard Day's Night, Help!*

Bow Wow (a.k.a. Lil' Bow Wow)—*Like Mike*

Cher—*Mask, Moonstruck, The Witches of Eastwick*

Jimmy Cliff—*The Harder They Come*

Bing Crosby—*Going My Way, Holiday Inn*

Ice Cube—*Boyz N the Hood, Higher Learning, Three Kings*

Whitney Houston—*The Bodyguard*

Janet Jackson—*Poetic Justice, Nutty Professor II: The Klumps*

Al Jolson—*The Jazz Singer*

Huey Lewis—*Short Cuts, Duets*

Courtney Love—*The People vs. Larry Flynt*

Lyle Lovett—*The Opposite of Sex, The Player*

Dean Martin—*Rio Bravo, Ocean's 11*

Liza Minnelli—*Cabaret, New York, New York, Arthur*

Willie Nelson—*Thief, The Electric Horseman, Wag the Dog*

Busta Rhymes—*Finding Forrester, Shaft*

Diana Ross—*Lady Sings the Blues, Mahogany*

Frank Sinatra—*From Here to Eternity, The Man With the Golden Arm, The Manchurian Candidate*

Will Smith—*Ali, Men in Black, Independence Day*

Barbra Streisand—*The Way We Were, Funny Girl, A Star Is Born, The Prince of Tides*

Mark Wahlberg—*The Perfect Storm, Rock Star, Boogie Nights, Three Kings*

Tom Waits—*Short Cuts, Mystery Men*

Dwight Yoakam—*Sling Blade, Panic Room*

worst
singers
turned
actors

worst singers turned actors

Sure, Elvis Presley made a lot of movies and he was fairly comfortable onscreen playing a sanitized version of himself—but they were all BAD movies. Have you tried to sit through *Blue Hawaii* or *Speedway* lately? You'll be squirming on the sofa within minutes. Not only that, but Presley spent so much time churning out these forgettable B-flicks that he lost his musical way for nearly a decade, only to redeem himself temporarily with "Suspicious Minds" and "In the Ghetto" before donning the white jumpsuit and forsaking all credibility. Elvis may be the most spectacular failure in the singer-turned-actor category, but he's far from being alone. The worst singers turned actors, and a few of their worst crimes against cinematic decency:

Lance Bass of 'NSYNC— *On the Line* (2001)

Björk— *Dancer in the Dark* (2000)

Jon Bon Jovi— *Pay It Forward* (2000), *No Looking Back* (1998), *Moonlight and Valentino* (1995)

Mariah Carey— *Glitter* (2001)

Roger Daltrey— *Tommy* (1975), *McVicar* (1980)

Neil Diamond— *The Jazz Singer* (1980), *Saving Silverman* (2001)

Bob Dylan— *Renaldo and Clara* (1978), *Pat Garrett and Billy the Kid* (1973)

Madonna—*Shanghai Surprise* (1986), *Body of Evidence* (1993), *The Next Best Thing* (2000), *Swept Away* (2002), *Who's That Girl?* * (1987)

Olivia Newton-John—*Xanadu* (1980), *Grease* (1978)

Luciano Pavarotti—*Yes, Giorgio* (1982)

Elvis Presley—*Fun in Acapulco* (1963), *Girls! Girls! Girls!* (1962), *Harum Scarum* (1965), *G.I. Blues* (1960)

Prince—*Purple Rain* (1984), *Under the Cherry Moon* (1986), *Graffiti Bridge* (1990)

Kid Rock—*Joe Dirt* (2001)

Britney Spears—*Crossroads* (2002)

*Note: Madonna sparkled in Evita *(1996) and she was OK in smallish roles in* Desperately Seeking Susan *(1985) and* A League of Their Own *(1992). It's when she's asked to carry a non-musical that she's in big trouble.*

closing
numbers

closing numbers

most movies end with the traditional white-on-black scroll of the credits, with everyone from the stars to the caterer to the animal stand-ins getting a mention while the music swells—but some films like to keep the fun rolling. If it's a comedy or a buddy movie, they'll often show a reel of bloopers and outtakes, with the stars laughing uproariously and punching each other on the shoulder as they blow their lines or play jokes on one another. (What I'd like to see is a blooper reel showing the star holed up in his trailer, doing lines of coke and bitching at his agent while some half-naked bimbo files her nails in the background. Of course, that sort of thing rarely happens on a movie set, right?) Occasionally, the closing-credit sequence will be augmented by a clever little "fortune cookie" or two, as when a bruised and battered Mr. Rooney limped onto the bus at the end of *Ferris Bueller's Day Off,* a hilarious scene that was followed by a fade to black, and then a cameo by Ferris himself, who looked at the camera, wondered what we were still doing there, and told us, "The movie's over. Go home."

In the late 1990s and early 2000s, another trend surfaced: the closing musical number, performed by the cast. Here's a partial list of movies in which the characters get together at the end to belt out a tune, either in a concert setting or in a music video.

Austin Powers: International Man of Mystery (1997)
Still in character, Mike Myers and the band "Ming Tea" pay

homage to 1960s dance-music shows with an original and catchy number, "BBC."

Coyote Ugly (2000)

LeAnn Rimes joins Piper Perabo, Tyra Banks, et al., on the top of the bar for a closing tune.

Jay and Silent Bob Strike Back (2001)

Morris Day and the Time reprise their big hit "Jungle Love."

Lost & Found (1999)

David Spade and Co. do "Groove Is in the Heart," by Dee-Lite.

Rat Race (2001)

Smash Mouth welcomes the cast onstage for a live version of "All Star."

Recess: School's Out (2001)

In this animated kids' flick, we get the voice of Robert Goulet, I kid you not, on "Green Tambourine," a trippy tune made popular by the Lemon Pipers in the 1960s.

Saving Silverman (2001)

Neil Diamond shares the stage with cast members Jack Black, Steve Zahn, Jason Biggs, Amanda Peet, and Lee Ermey, who played the sadistic drill sergeant in Full Metal Jacket but these days would show up at the opening of an envelope if somebody paid him for it.

closing numbers

Shrek (2001)

The green ogre with a heart of gold and his donkey sidekick lead their fractured fairy tale friends in an update of the Monkees' "I'm a Believer."

There's Something About Mary (1998)

Ben Stiller, Cameron Diaz, and Brett "F-f-farver," among others, perform a sing-along version of the Foundations' "Build Me Up Buttercup."

10 bad
songs put to
use in
good
movies

10 bad songs put to use in good movies

"Atlantis" by Donovan—*GoodFellas*

One of the most pretentious and silly spoken-word pop hits ever becomes poignant and haunting when it plays in the background while gangsters Robert De Niro, Ray Liotta, and Joe Pesci stomp a rival mobster to death.

"Brand New Key" by Melanie—*Boogie Nights*

When Heather "Rollergirl" Graham took off all her clothes and skated over to Mark Wahlberg, I suddenly realized, "I LOVE THIS SONG!!!"

"Danke Schoen," Wayne Newton—*Ferris Bueller's Day Off*

Matthew Broderick sings this camp hit in the shower as he starts his day and later lip-synchs it during the "German Day" parade in downtown Chicago.

"I Got You Babe," Sonny & Cher—*Groundhog Day*

This is the tune that Bill Murray's character hears on his clock radio as he repeatedly wakes up on the same morning in Groundhog Day.

"In-A-Gadda-Da-Vidda," Iron Butterfly—*Manhunter*

Used as the backdrop for the final, violent confrontation in Manhunter, *the first movie about Hannibal the Cannibal.*

"I Say a Little Prayer," Burt Bacharach—*My Best Friend's Wedding*

The launching point for the ridiculous but fabulously entertaining sing-along number by Rupert Everett and Co. in My Best Friend's Wedding.

"Killing Me Softly," Roberta Flack—*About a Boy*

Focal point for a climactic scene featuring Hugh Grant in About a Boy, *one of the most charming films of 2002.*

"My Sharona," The Knack—*Reality Bites*

Gets Winona Ryder dancing in a convenience store in Reality Bites. *And she doesn't steal a thing!*

"(I Can't Get No) Satisfaction," Devo—Casino

The original "Satisfaction" by the Rolling Stones was a classic, but Devo's remake was just plain goofy. Once again, though, Scorsese finds a seemingly disposable song and puts it to good use.

√ "Stuck in the Middle With You," Stealer's Wheel—*Reservoir Dogs*

Michael Madsen turns up the radio and grooves to the sound of this once-forgotten 1970s hit as he slices the ear off a cop.

10 sure
signs a movie
character
is
doomed

10 sure signs a movie character is doomed

Woody Allen is one of the few directors whose subjects consistently go to the movies and talk about the movies. Characters in other movies hardly ever *go* to movies, unless they're making out in a drive-in theater or running through a crowded multiplex in an effort to shake off the bad guys. Maybe that's why so many movie people are blissfully unaware that they're never going to make it to the end of the story, even though they've been marked with one of the sure signs a character has been doomed.

But as film buffs, we recognize the moment when it becomes painfully clear that a certain character has been marked for death. For some, it's when they say or do the wrong thing—the thing that will get them killed in the next reel. For others, the very nature of their existence tells us that they will not be around for long.

Sure signs a character is doomed:

1. **The researcher who is working late in the police lab and calls up the lead cop and says, "I know who did it! Meet me at the crime scene at 11 tonight." After hanging up the phone, the researcher will be greeted by a visitor who is not shown on camera and will say, "Hey, what are YOU doing here?" And then the researcher will get whacked.**

2. **The spunky little kid or the wizened old soul who befriends a main character in a hospital has no chance.**

We'll find out the kid (or the old-timer) has died when the main character stops in to pay a visit, only to see a nurse's aide stripping the bed. Nothing says death in a hospital scene like a nurse's aide stripping the bed.

3. The fresh-faced soldier who talks endlessly about his girlfriend, looks longingly at her photo every night, and tells everyone, "We're going to have a baby!" will be coming home in a body bag.

4. The pregnant young wife who looks at her husband with pure love and says "I've never been happier in my entire life" has no chance of making it out of the movie alive.

5. Another type who has no chance of surviving the movie: The anonymous henchman who exists only to fight the superhero and never realizes that it would be better to team up with his fellow anonymous henchmen for a group attack rather than waiting his turn to be defeated by the hero. (See the *Austin Powers* movies.)

6. Of course, all lusty teenagers in the *Friday the 13th, Halloween*, or *Nightmare on Elm Street* movies will be sliced and diced to pieces, usually after they've just made love or gone skinny-dipping.

7. The popular veteran cop who has travel brochures on his desk and is a week away from retirement—he's never going to see that condo in Arizona, is he?

8. If a team of criminals or investigators has one black guy played by an actor who's not as famous as anyone else,

10 sure signs a movie character is doomed

that guy has no chance. (As explained in *Undercover Brother*.)

9. The bad guy is locked in a life-and-death clinch with the good guy, when suddenly a gun goes off. We see the look of shock on the good guy's face as he falls away—but of course it's the bad guy who's been shot in the gut.

10. Wise old-timers in the form of janitors, next-door neighbors, retired athletes, or inmates who have been locked up for 50 years—they're bound to croak, usually in the arms of their young protégé, who says, "Don't you die on me now!" as if it's up to the old guy.

bad films featuring *Seinfeld* cast members

bad films featuring *Seinfeld* cast members

erry Seinfeld has always been a TV and nightclub guy—his only "feature" film is the 2002 documentary *Comedian*, which chronicles his return to stand-up—but his three co-stars have collectively done more than a dozen movies, most of them not nearly as interesting as "Rochelle, Rochelle." Granted, Jason Alexander was effective as Richard Gere's creepy lawyer friend in *Pretty Woman* and Julia Louis-Dreyfus did some nice work in the Woody Allen films *Hannah and Her Sisters* and *Deconstructing Harry*, but most of the films with one or more of the *Seinfeld* supporting trio have been utterly disposable.

Jason Alexander

Blankman (1994)

Coneheads (1993)

Dunston Checks In (1996)

I Don't Buy Kisses Anymore (1992)

North (1994)

Julia Louis-Dreyfus

Fathers' Day (1997)

North (1994)

Soul Man (1986)

Michael Richards

Airheads (1994)

Coneheads (1993)

Problem Child (1990)

Transylvania 6-5000 (1985)

UHF (1989)

Unstrung Heroes (1995)

the worst sequels of all time

the worst sequels of all time

ost sequels are like Frank Sinatra, Jr.—from conception, there was just no chance of equaling the original. But some films with "*Part 2*" or "*The Next Chapter*" are so odious, so egregiously awful, that they taint our memories of the films from which they were spawned.

I hate these movies.

Now, there's no point in listing the stinko franchises—for example, all the "*Police Academy*" and "*Chucky*" and "*Poison Ivy*" and "*Friday the 13th*" movies—seeing as how the originals weren't any good in the first place. (Did anyone expect *Cyborg Cop III* to be any good?) The sequels on this list are more offensively mediocre because they followed some good, and in some cases great, films.

102 Dalmatians (2000)

Another 48 Hrs. (1990)

Arthur 2: On the Rocks (1988)

The Bad News Bears Go to Japan (1978)

Batman & Robin (1997)

Beneath the Planet of the Apes (1970)

Beverly Hills Cop III (1994)

Blues Brothers 2000 (1998)

Caddyshack II (1988)

Cannonball Run II (1984)

Escape From L.A. (1996)

Exorcist II: The Heretic (1977)

Grease 2 (1982)

Hannibal (2001)

I Still Know What You Did Last Summer (1998)

Jaws 3-D (1983)

Jaws: the Revenge (1987)

Lethal Weapon 4 (1998)

Look Who's Talking Too (1990)

Major League: Back to the Minors (1998)

Mission: Impossible II (2000)

The Next Karate Kid (1994)

Psycho III (1986)

Rambo III (1988)

Robocop 2 (1990)

Rocky V (1990)

Scary Movie 2 (2001)

Speed 2: Cruise Control (1997)

Staying Alive (1983)

The Sting II (1983)

Superman III (1983)

Teen Wolf Too (1987)

3 Men and a Little Lady (1990)

Trail of the Pink Panther (1982)

decent
sequels

decent sequels

 ost sequels are terrible. These weren't.

American Pie 2 (2001)

Austin Powers in Goldmember (2002)

Austin Powers: The Spy Who Shagged Me (1999)

Batman Returns (1992)

Book of Shadows: Blair Witch 2 (2000)

Bride of Frankenstein (1935)

The Color of Money (1986)

Conquest of the Planet of the Apes (1972)

Dawn of the Dead (1978)

Die Hard 2 (1990)

The Godfather: Part II (1974)

The Good, the Bad and the Ugly (1966)

Indiana Jones and the Last Crusade (1989)

Indiana Jones and the Temple of Doom (1984)

Mad Max 2: The Road Warrior (1981)

Mad Max Beyond Thunderdome (1985)

Magnum Force (1973)

Return of the Jedi (1983)

Rocky II (1979)

Scream 2 (1997)

Stuart Little 2 (2002)

Terminator 2: Judgment Day (1991)

sequels
that have
equaled
or
bettered
the
original

sequels that have equaled or bettered the original

Aliens (1986)

Babe: Pig in the City (1998)

The Empire Strikes Back (1980)

The Godfather, Part II (1974)

Toy Story 2 (1999)

the 40 **worst** movies I've **ever** seen

the 40 worst movies I've ever seen

can't compile a list of the worst movies in history because I haven't seen every movie in history, and I won't go so far as to list the 100 lousiest films I've seen because reliving that many bad experiences would plunge me into deep therapy for years—but I will give you my list of the 40 movies that linger in the back chambers of my memory vault like a plate of cheese left behind a radiator in a fleabag hotel. They come to you in alphabetical order because at some point, awful is just awful.

1. *Arthur 2: On the Rocks* (1988)

Dudley Moore's title character was one of the funniest drunks ever—but when he sobered up, he lost his sense of humor.

2. *The Babe Ruth Story* (1948)

The John Goodman version of the Bambino's story wasn't much better, but at least Goodman looked like he'd held a bat in his hands once or twice before filming commenced. You couldn't say the same of William Bendix.

3. *BAPS* (1997)

This exploitative, embarrassing, and appalling comedy will dog Oscar-winner Halle Berry for the rest of her days.

4. BASEketball (1998)

The best thing about this movie is Jenny McCarthy. And when the best thing you can say about a movie is that Jenny McCarthy is the best thing in the movie, that's a bad movie.

5. Battlefield Earth (2000)

The real danger of Scientology is that John Travolta may some-day make another movie based on the writings of L. Ron Hubbard.

6. Bio-Dome (1996)

A Pauly Shore vehicle based on the little-remembered Biosphere 2 project. Gee, I wonder where it went wrong.

7. Bob & Carol & Ted & Alice (1969)

Dumb & Painful & Lame & Boring.

8. Chitty Chitty Bang Bang (1968)

Sputter sputter klunk klunk.

9. Crash (1996)

A journey inside the minds of people who get sexually aroused by automobile accidents. As if anyone would want to take such a trip.

10. Death Becomes Her (1992)

A shrill, ugly comedy with bad, overbaked performances from the normally reliable Meryl Streep, Bruce Willis, and Goldie Hawn.

11. Don't Tell Her It's Me (1990)

A morbidly unaffecting melodrama starring Steve Guttenberg as a terminally ill cancer patient who falls in love.

the 40 worst movies I've ever seen

12. *Exit to Eden* (1994)

A sex comedy starring Rosie O'Donnell in leather and chains. Now, if it had been a horror movie . . .

13. *Forget Paris* (1995)

Billy Crystal is an NBA referee (now there's a profession for a romantic lead) who falls in love with Debra Winger. In one extended scene, she gets a pigeon stuck in her hair. Neither Winger nor the pigeon looks pleased.

14. *Freddy Got Fingered* (2001)

Tom Green is the Pauly Shore of the 21st century—only more disgusting and even less funny. His momentary fame is one of the great mysteries of modern show business. (For that matter, so was his brief marriage to Drew Barrymore.)

15. *Glitter* (2001)

Mariah Carey's star vehicle should have been titled "Flash-dunce."

16. *Godzilla* (1998)

Redefines the term "disaster movie."

17. *The Great Race* (1965)

Just because the cast is filled with recognizable faces and

there's lots of frantic music doesn't mean it can't be unspeakably dull.

18. *The Green Berets* (1968)

Shameless propaganda about U.S. involvement in Vietnam. Looks like it was produced by the Department of Defense and directed by Barry Goldwater.

19. *Indecent Proposal* (1993)

Cynical, pretentious crap has Robert Redford paying Woody Harrelson $1 million so he can sleep with Demi Moore and her ridiculous breast implants.

20. *Ishtar* (1987)

As is the case with Heaven's Gate, the stories about the making of this disaster are infinitely more entertaining than the end product.

21. *Jinxed!* (1982)

Bette Midler and Ken Wahl—now there's a sizzling hot couple!

22. *Johnny Be Good* (1988)

Anthony Michael Hall, famous for playing skinny but smart geeks in John Hughes movies, gets weirdly beefed up to play an obnoxious football star.

23. *Leonard Part 6* (1987)

There's an urban legend that Bill Cosby bought the rights to all the old Little Rascals movies just so he could keep them off TV. That's not true—but Cosby SHOULD buy and burn up every print of Leonard Part 6.

the 40 worst movies I've ever seen

24. *Link* (1986)

A chimp lusts after Elisabeth Shue. See what happens when you break up with the Karate Kid?

25. *Listen to Me* (1989)

Heavy-handed drama about a college debate team, starring Kirk Growing Pains Cameron.

26. *Man Trouble* (1992)

Jack Nicholson and Ellen Barkin look hopelessly lost throughout this deadly comedy.

27. *Me and Him* (1987)

Griffin Dunne has a running dialogue with his penis. The penis gets the best lines.

28. *My Stepmother Is an Alien* (1988)

Apparently they don't have acting lessons in outer space.

29. *1941* (1979)

Proof that even Steven Spielberg can make a bomb, in more ways than one.

30. *North* (1994)

Of all the films on this list, North may be the most difficult to watch from start to finish. I've tried twice, and I've failed. Do yourself a favor and don't even attempt it. Life is too short.

31. *Oh, Heavenly Dog!* (1980)

Benji out-acts Chevy Chase.

32. *The Postman* (1997)

Kevin Costner as a futuristic mailman. Who knew stamps would be $3,000 each!

33. *Problem Child* (1990)

John Ritter adopts a charmless brat.

34. *Rambo III* (1988)

The first "Rambo" was an interesting examination of a disenfranchised Vietnam vet who can't adjust to a non-violent life in the States. But by the third installment, Sylvester Stallone had turned Rambo into a superhero killing machine spouting embarrassing speeches about what it means to be an American.

35. *Speed 2* (1997)

Set the sequel to Speed on a big slow ship, that's a great idea! Say what you will about Keanu Reeves's brainpower, but he had the good sense not to sign up for this turgid sequel.

36. *The Sweetest Thing* (2002)

Cameron Diaz, Christina Applegate, and Selma Blair star in a gross-out road-trip comedy that proves a movie starring three women and written by a woman can be just as disgusting and lamebrained as anything the guys can do.

the 40 worst movies I've ever seen

37. *Tomcats* (2001)
Hateful, inane comedy about idiotic guys who spend every waking moment trying to nail stupid bimbos.

38. *Tommy* (1975)
Garish adaptation of the Who's musical reaches its low point when Ann-Margret slithers in baked beans.

39. *Weekend at Bernie's* (1989)
Corpse comedy is D.O.A.

40. *Where the Buffalo Roam* (1980)
Based on this disaster and Fear and Loathing in Las Vegas, *I'd have to conclude that Hunter S. Thompson's lunatic genius is unfilmable.*

5 things that **happen** when a **wrongly** accused **fugitive** walks into a **bar,** a **restaurant,** or a convenience **store**

5 things that happen when a wrongly accused fugitive walks into a bar, a restaurant, or a convenience store

1. A television will be turned on, and the news will be playing.
2. The fugitive will glance nervously at the TV and then order a drink or a pack of smokes.
3. The newscaster will start reading a story about the fugitive, with a mug shot of the fugitive prominently displayed.
4. A customer will glance at the fugitive and then back at the TV.
5. Just as the customer realizes the fugitive is RIGHT THERE, he turns—and the fugitive is gone, the door swinging in his wake.

actresses
who
have played
prostitutes

actresses who have played prostitutes

 or every actor who has played a drunk, there's an actress who has portrayed a hooker.

Drew Barrymore, *Bad Girls* (1994)

Kim Basinger, *L.A. Confidential* (1997)

Leslie Caron, *The L-Shaped Room* (1962)

Julie Christie, *McCabe & Mrs. Miller* (1971)

Joan Chen, *The Hunted* (1995)

Joan Crawford, *Rain* (1932)

Jamie Lee Curtis, *Trading Places* (1983)

Julie Delpy, *Killing Zoe* (1994)

Catherine Deneuve, *Belle de Jour* (1968)

Marlene Dietrich, *Shanghai Express* (1932)

Linda Fiorentino, *Jade* (1995)

Bridget Fonda, *Scandal* (1989)

Jane Fonda, *Klute* (1971)

Jodie Foster, *Taxi Driver* (1976)

Greta Garbo, *Anna Christie* (1930)

Heather Graham, *From Hell* (2001)

Melanie Griffith, *Milk Money* (1994)

Helen Hayes, *The Sin of Madelon Claudet* (1931)

Audrey Hepburn, *Breakfast at Tiffany's* (1961) (Hey—she got $50 to go to the powder room, for crying out loud.)

Barbara Hershey, *The Last Temptation of Christ* (1988)

Shirley Jones, *Elmer Gantry* (1960)

Milla Jovovich, *He Got Game* (1998)

Jennifer Jason Leigh, *Last Exit to Brooklyn* (1989), among others

Lucy Liu, *Bang* (1995)

Myrna Loy, *Penthouse* (1933)

Andie MacDowell, *Bad Girls* (1994)

Shirley MacLaine, *Some Came Running* (1958), *Two Mules for Sister Sara* (1970), and *Irma la Douce* (1963)

Melina Mercouri, *Never on Sunday* (1960)

Gwyneth Paltrow, *Hard Eight* (1996)

Michelle Pfeiffer, *Into the Night* (1985)

Donna Reed, *From Here to Eternity* (1953)

Julia Roberts, *Pretty Woman* (1990)

Theresa Russell, *Whore* (1991)

Susan Sarandon, *Pretty Baby* (1978)

Brooke Shields, *Pretty Baby* (1978)

Elisabeth Shue, *Leaving Las Vegas* (1995)

Mira Sorvino, *Mighty Aphrodite* (1995)

Sharon Stone, *Casino* (1995)

Madeleine Stowe, *Bad Girls* (1994)

Gloria Swanson, *Sadie Thompson* (1928)

Elizabeth Taylor, *Butterfield 8* (1960)

Claire Trevor, *Dead End* (1937)

Rachel Ward, *Sharky's Machine* (1981)

Debra Winger, *Cannery Row* (1982)

best
porn
titles based on
legit
movies

best porn titles based on legit movies

6 Lays, 7 Nights

As Good as Head Gets

Ass Ventura: The Crack Detective

The Beaverly Hillbillies

Bonfire of the Panties

Buffy, the Vampire Layer

Cape Rear

Cliffbanger

A Clockwork Orgy

Done in 60 Seconds

Driving Miss Daisy Crazy

Dumb and Done Her

Edward Penishands

E-Three: The Extra Testicle

Face Jam

The Flintbones

For Your Thighs Only

Forrest Hump

Free My Willy

Glad He Ate Her

Good Will Humping

Hannah Does Her Sisters

Inspect Her Gadget

Jurassic Pork

A League of Their Moan

On Golden Blonde

Pocahontass

Porn on the 4th of July

Position: Impossible

Romancing the Bone

Saving Ryan's Privates

Schindler's Fist

Snatch Adams

There's Someone on Mary

There Were 12 Men But They Weren't Angry

The Three Musket Queers

Was That as Good as It Gets?

White Men Can't Hump

Who's Eating Gilbert Grape?

You Have Male

acting
drunk

acting drunk

just as nearly every major actress will play a hooker at some point in her career, most actors will have to act drunk at least once in their careers. It could be argued that movie heroes from Rick in *Casablanca* to Bluto in *Animal House* had serious drinking problems, but those were movies with characters who happened to drink a lot—they weren't specifically ABOUT the alcoholism of the main characters. The following list, which is by no means complete, is restricted to roles in which the character is defined, and often consumed, by his alcoholism.

Ben Affleck, *Bounce* (2000)

Kevin Bacon, *Diner* (1982)

Wallace Beery, *The Champ* (1931)

Jeff Bridges, *8 Million Ways to Die* (1986)

Nicolas Cage, *Leaving Las Vegas* (1995)

James Coburn, *Affliction* (1997)

Bing Crosby, *The Country Girl* (1954)

Matt Damon, *The Legend of Bagger Vance* (2000)

Michael Douglas, *Basic Instinct* (1992)

Robert Duvall, *Tender Mercies* (1983)

Albert Finney, *Under the Volcano* (1984)

Morgan Freeman, *High Crimes* (2002)

Dennis Hopper, *Hoosiers* (1986)

Samuel L. Jackson, *Changing Lanes* (2002)

Michael Keaton, *Clean and Sober* (1988)

Jack Lemmon, *Days of Wine and Roses* (1962)

Lee Marvin, *Cat Ballou* (1965)

James Mason, *A Star Is Born* (1954)

Ray Milland, *The Lost Weekend* (1945)

Dudley Moore, *Arthur* (1981)

Paul Newman, *The Verdict* (1982)

Jack Nicholson, *Ironweed* (1987)

Laurence Olivier, *The Entertainer* (1960)

Peter O'Toole, *My Favorite Year* (1982)

Al Pacino, *Scent of a Woman* (1992)

John Ritter, *Skin Deep* (1989)

Jason Robards, *Long Day's Journey Into Night* (1962)

Mickey Rourke, *Barfly* (1987)

Jimmy Stewart, *Harvey* (1950)

Bruce Willis, *Die Hard: With a Vengeance* (1995)

James Woods, *Curse of the Starving Class* (1994)

from small screen to big disaster

from small screen to big disaster

hollywood has been making movies based on television shows since the advent of TV, with early efforts such as *The Life of Riley* in 1949 and *Our Miss Brooks* in 1956—but this generally bad idea didn't explode into a big-ass trend until the early 1990s, when it seemed as if half the creative forces in town threw up their hands at the same time and said: "Screw it, we're out of ideas. Let's just start flipping through back issues of *TV Guide*!" In the first five years of the 1990s, we were subjected to this deadly roster of terrible films, most based on TV shows or characters that weren't any good in the first place:

The Addams Family (1991)

Addams Family Values (1993)

The Beverly Hillbillies (1993)

Boris and Natasha (1992)

Car 54, Where Are You? (1994)

Coneheads (1993)

Dennis the Menace (1993)

The Flintstones (1994)

It's Pat (1994)

Jetsons: The Movie (1990)

Maverick (1994)

Star Trek 6: The Undiscovered Country (1991)

Stuart Saves His Family (1995)

Twin Peaks: Fire Walk With Me (1992)

Now that would make for one ugly film festival. To be fair, there were a few entertaining theatrical adaptations of TV hits during that period, including the *Wayne's World* films, the *Brady Bunch* takeoffs and *The Fugitive*, perhaps the best movie ever based on a TV series. But films such as *Boris and Natasha* and *Car 54, Where Are You?* are so bad that you can't even find them at the bottom of the bargain video bins at Wal-Mart.

In addition to the aforementioned disasters, some other other god-awful films based on TV shows or characters:

The Adventures of Rocky and Bullwinkle (2000)

Bean (1997)

Charlie's Angels (2000)

Dragnet (1987)

The Flintstones in Viva Rock Vegas (2000)

Hey Arnold! The Movie (2002)

The Ladies Man (2000)

Leave It to Beaver (1997)

Lost in Space (1998)

A Night at the Roxbury (1998)

The Powerpuff Girls (2002)

Scooby-Doo (2002)

Sgt. Bilko (1996)

15 movies with **wise-cracking but caring gay best friends** who usually live **right down the hall and** are **always available** to lend a shoulder **to cry on**

15 movies with wisecracking but caring gay best friends who usually live right down the hall and are always available to lend a shoulder to cry on

Adam's Rib

David Wayne as Katharine Hepburn's wisecracking but caring gay friend. (They couldn't say he was gay back in 1949, but please. Watch the movie.)

As Good as It Gets

Greg Kinnear as Jack Nicholson's wisecracking but ultimately caring gay neighbor.

Blast From the Past

Dave Foley as Alicia Silverstone's wisecracking but caring gay housemate.

Bridget Jones's Diary

James Callis as Renée Zellweger's wisecracking but caring gay friend.

Flawless

Philip Seymour Hoffman as Robert De Niro's wisecracking gay neighbor, who becomes his best friend.

Frankie and Johnny

Nathan Lane as Michelle Pfeiffer's wisecracking but caring gay neighbor.

My Best Friend's Wedding

Rupert Everett as Julia Roberts' wisecracking but caring gay best friend.

The Next Best Thing

Rupert Everett as Madonna's wisecracking but caring gay best friend.

The Object of My Affection

Paul Rudd as Jennifer Aniston's wisecracking but caring gay best friend, who's so great that she falls in love with him, even though he's her wisecracking but caring GAY best friend.

Prince of Tides

George Carlin as Nick Nolte's wisecracking but caring gay neighbor.

Reality Bites

Steve Zahn as Winona Ryder's wisecracking but caring gay housemate.

Silkwood

Cher as Meryl Streep's wisecracking but caring gay best friend.

Single White Female

Peter Friedman as Bridget Fonda's wisecracking but caring gay neighbor.

Sweet November

Jason Isaacs as Charlize Theron's wisecracking but caring gay neighbor.

15 movies with wisecracking but caring gay best friends who usually live right down the hall and are always available to lend a shoulder to cry on

Woman on Top

  Harold Perrineau, Jr., as Penélope Cruz's wisecracking but caring gay best friend.

meg ryan's

ryan's

movie

names

meg ryan's movie names

When Meg Ryan scrunches up her nose and flips her hair and lights up the room with her smile, she just looks like a Maggie or a Kate or a Katherine, doesn't she? At least that's what a lot of filmmakers must believe, based on this partial list of Ryan's character names:

> *Addicted to Love*—Maggie
>
> *Armed and Dangerous*—Maggie
>
> *City of Angels*—Maggie
>
> *Flesh and Bone*—Kay
>
> *French Kiss*—Kate
>
> *I.Q.*—Catherine
>
> *Kate & Leopold*—Kate
>
> *Restoration*—Katharine
>
> *You've Got Mail*—Kathleen

[Note: Meg Ryan's real name is Margaret Mary Emily Anne Hyra.]

a kiss
is just
a kiss

a kiss is just a kiss

f you're an aspiring actress hoping to make it in feature films, be prepared to kiss a girl on camera. I'm not saying you'll be playing a lesbian—it just means that men still dominate the ranks of screenwriters, producers, and directors in Hollywood, and men love to see women kiss, so they'll find just about any excuse to get two females kissing or even doing some light fondling in a film, whether it's integral to the plot or not. Consider that Winona Ryder, who by all accounts is a heterosexual woman, has engaged in three girl-on-girl kissing scenes in films—plus she smooched with Jennifer Aniston on a "very special episode" of *Friends*. (In this case, "very special episode" is code talk for "Gentlemen, start your Tivos.") Can you imagine a male star about Ryder's age—say, Ben Affleck or Matt Damon—agreeing to do that many gay kisses?

Me neither. That's because most men find it highly erotic when two women kiss, whereas most women aren't all that interested in seeing two men smooching.

Hollywood knows this. That's why the following list of actresses who have kissed onscreen is so extensive.

Sarah Michelle Gellar and Selma Blair in *Cruel Intentions* (1999)

Susan Sarandon and Catherine Deneuve in *The Hunger* (1983)

Denise Richards and Neve Campbell in *Wild Things* (1998)

Laura Elena Harring and Naomi Watts in *Mulholland Dr.* (2001)

Piper Perabo and Jessica Paré in *Lost and Delirious* (2001)

Salma Hayek and Jeanne Tripplehorn in *Time Code* (2000)

Anne Heche and Joan Chen in *Wild Side* (1995)

Heather Graham and Lisa Zane in *Terrified* (1995)

Mariel Hemingway and Patrice Donnelly in *Personal Best* (1982)

Emmanuelle Seigner and Kristin Scott Thomas in *Bitter Moon* (1992)

Debra Winger and Theresa Russell in *Black Widow* (1987)

Gina Gershon and Jennifer Tilly in *Bound* (1996)

Claire Forlani and Amanda Detmer in *Boys and Girls* (2000)

Winona Ryder and Sadie Frost in *Bram Stoker's Dracula* (1992)

Natasha Lyonne and Clea DuVall in *But I'm a Cheerleader* (1999)

Ione Skye and Meg Tilly in *Carmilla* (1990)

Winona Ryder and unnamed actress in *Celebrity* (1998)

Joey Lauren Adams and Carmen Lee in *Chasing Amy* (1997)

Jane March and Lesley Ann Warren in *Color of Night* (1994)

Rosanna Arquette and Holly Hunter in *Crash* (1996)

Helen Shaver and Patricia Charbonneau in *Desert Hearts* (1985)

Brigitte Bardot and Jane Birkin in *Don Juan 73* (1973)

Liv Tyler and Kate Hudson in *Dr. T & the Women* (2000)

Charlotte Lewis and Alyssa Milano in *Embrace of the Vampire* (1994)

Uma Thurman and Rain Phoenix in *Even Cowgirls Get the Blues* (1993)

Tilda Swinton and Karen Sillas in *Female Perversions* (1996)

Dominique Swain and Tara Reid in *Girl* (1998)

Angelina Jolie and Winona Ryder in *Girl, Interrupted* (1999)

Kate Capshaw and Elle Macpherson in *A Girl Thing* (2001)
   (episode in cable movie)

Kate Winslet and Melanie Lynskey in *Heavenly Creatures* (1994)

Uma Thurman and Maria de Medeiros in *Henry & June* (1990)

Jennifer Connelly and Kristy Swanson in *Higher Learning* (1995)

a kiss is just a kiss

Jodie Foster and Nastassja Kinski in *Hotel New Hampshire* (1984)

Michelle Williams and Chloë Sevigny in *If These Walls Could Talk 2* (2000) (episode in cable movie)

Radha Mitchell and Frances O'Connor in *Love and Other Catastrophes* (1996)

Peta Wilson and Ellen Barkin in *Mercy* (2000)

Kelly McGillis and Susie Porter in *The Monkey's Mask* (2000)

Raquel Welch and Farrah Fawcett in *Myra Breckinridge* (1970)

Pamela Anderson and Elizabeth Low in *Naked Souls* (1995)

Mia Kirshner and Dominique Swain in *New Best Friend* (2002)

Jennifer Aniston and Dagmara Dominczyk in *Rock Star* (2001)

Gwyneth Paltrow and unnamed actress in *The Royal Tenenbaums* (2001)

when **men** kiss **men**

when men kiss men

When a woman kisses a woman in a movie, it might be an integral scene that advances the story—or it might just be two hot chicks kissing. But when a man kisses a man, it's almost always done as a major plot point, or to get squirming laughs from the audience. Major stars are certainly willing to portray homosexuals, e.g., Tom Hanks and Antonio Banderas in *Philadelphia,* but they rarely agree to actually demonstrate any kind of physical affection. Robin Williams and Nathan Lane swished all over the screen in *The Birdcage,* but they hardly ever touched one another.

But there are some brave exceptions:

Mike Myers and Nathan Lane in *Austin Powers in Goldmember* (2002)

Seann William Scott and Jason Biggs in *American Pie 2* (2001)

Timothy Olyphant and Chris Wiehl in *Broken Hearts Club* (2000)

Peter Dante and Jonathan Loughran in *Big Daddy* (1999)

Chris Cooper and Kevin Spacey in *American Beauty* (1999)

Matt Stone and Trey Parker in *BASEketball* (1998)

Paul Rudd and Amo Gulinello in *The Object of My Affection* (1998)

Tom Selleck and Kevin Kline in *In & Out* (1997)

Steven Weber and Michael T. Weiss in *Jeffrey* (1995)

Keanu Reeves and William Richert in *My Own Private Idaho* (1991)

Michael Caine and Christopher Reeve in *Deathtrap* (1982)

Harry Hamlin and Michael Ontkean in *Making Love* (1982)

the 25 best sports movies of all time

(in order of preference)

the 25 best sports movies of all time (in order of preference)

1. *The Natural* (1984)
2. *Raging Bull* (1980)
3. *Rocky* (1976)
4. *Bull Durham* (1988)
5. *Field of Dreams* (1989)
6. *Heaven Can Wait* (1978)
7. *Hoosiers* (1986)
8. *Jerry Maguire* (1996)
9. *Tin Cup* (1996)
10. *Bang the Drum Slowly* (1973)
11. *North Dallas Forty* (1979)
12. *Any Given Sunday* (1999)
13. *Pride of the Yankees* (1942)
14. *Slap Shot* (1977)
15. *When We Were Kings* (1996)
16. *Major League* (1989)
17. *All the Right Moves* (1983)
18. *Downhill Racer* (1969)
19. *Rudy* (1993)
20. *Hoop Dreams* (1994)
21. *Blue Chips* (1994)
22. *Kingpin* (1996)

23. *Semi-Tough* (1978)
24. *White Men Can't Jump* (1992)
25. *The Longest Yard* (1974)

Honorable mention: The original made-for-TV movie Brian's Song, *starring James Caan and Billy Dee Williams.*

the 25 worst sports movies of all time

(in alphabetical order)

the 25 worst sports movies of all time (in alphabetical order)

Air Bud (1997)

The Babe (1992)

The Babe Ruth Story (1948)

The Bad News Bears Go to Japan (1978)

The Champ (1979)

The Cutting Edge (1992)

D3: The Mighty Ducks (1996)

Days of Thunder (1990)

Driven (2001)

The Fan (1996)

Fast Break (1979)

Fear Strikes Out (1957)

The Fish That Saved Pittsburgh (1979)

Ice Castles (1978)

Johnny Be Good (1988)

Juwanna Mann (2002)

Kansas City Bomber (1972)

The Legend of Bagger Vance (2000)

Major League: Back to the Minors (1998)

Oxford Blues (1984)

The Replacements (2000)

Rocky V (1990)

The Slugger's Wife (1985)

Space Jam (1996)

Youngblood (1986)

movies in which **Tom Cruise obscures** his face with **grotesque** makeup or a **mask**

movies in which Tom Cruise obscures his face with grotesque makeup or a mask

for four consecutive years, starting in 1999, the world's most popular movie star has selected roles in which he has hidden his famous visage behind a mask or has worn prosthetics and makeup to distort his features. We'll leave it to his Scientology friends or his good friend Oprah to examine what's behind this trend.

The movies, and the facial disguise of choice:

Eyes Wide Shut (1999)

Cruise visits a costume shop and purchases a mask that he wears to a mysterious orgy at a mansion.

Mission: Impossible II (2000)

Cruise wears a mask to conceal his true identity—that of a big movie star getting paid millions to do a lame sequel.

Vanilla Sky (2001)

After his face is shattered in a car crash, Cruise wears a mask to hide from the world, and to keep the world from seeing his twisted and scarred features. In other scenes, we see the results of the car crash, as Cruise's face is nearly unrecognizable beneath all the makeup.

Minority Report (2002)

As a futuristic cop on the run, Cruise takes a pill that temporarily distorts his face and makes him look like an old man. He also spends part of the film wearing a bandage over his eyes.

when movies go to class

when movies go to class

t hardly matters if we're talking grade school, high school, or college—when we're in a classroom, we know certain things will probably happen.

1. If two students in the back of the class are talking, the teacher will always catch them and say something like, "All right, Mister Star-of-the-Movie, perhaps you can enlighten us. What was Blake trying to say?"

2. When the new kid in town is the only one in class who knows the answer to a question, he'll be heckled by the jock—but the smart pretty girl will tell the jock to pipe down, and she will smile encouragingly at the new kid. This will cause the jock to mouth the words "You're a dead man!" to the new kid.

3. The bell always rings right after a dramatic confrontation or a humorous moment in class, and as the students race for the door, the teacher will struggle to be heard above the din, telling the kids: "Don't forget, your term papers have to be on my desk Monday morning! No exceptions!"

4. If the camera lingers on an empty desk, it doesn't mean someone is sick. It means someone is dead.

5. Substitute teachers are always good-looking.

6. Even in the 21st century, even at the finest private institutions, all teachers still use a blackboard and chalk.

7. All high school science classes have only one lab exercise: dissecting frogs.

8. If a college professor is having an affair with a student, the professor will be particularly tough on the student in class.

9. Even in the inner city, classrooms are never overcrowded. There are usually about 15 kids per class, but two thirds never say a word because they're extras and they don't have speaking parts.

10. If a teacher reads an outstanding essay in class, the author always turns out to be the "least likely" candidate.

uncoordinated

acting

uncoordinated acting

from Babe Ruth to Wilt Chamberlain to Joe Namath to Michael Jordan to Shaquille O'Neal, a lot of top athletes have proved to be terrible actors. Then again, a lot of actors are bad athletes, and no amount of editing in the world can save them from looking dorky and awkward onscreen. Keep in mind that we're not judging the quality of the acting or the film itself, but the physical mechanics of the stars in their attempt to come across as legitimate athletes. For example, Tim Robbins was funny and convincing as a horny but good-hearted rube in *Bull Durham*, but on the mound, he just didn't cut it.

William Bendix as Babe Ruth in *The Babe Ruth Story* (1948)

John Favreau as a pro linebacker in *The Replacements* (2000)

Brendan Fraser as a rookie phenom in *The Scout* (1994)

John Goodman as Babe Ruth in *The Babe* (1992)

Ray Liotta as Shoeless Joe Jackson in *Field of Dreams* (1989)
(Jackson threw right and batted left, but in the movie Liotta was a lefty who batted from the right side.)

Rob Lowe as a hockey star in *Youngblood* (1986), **an amateur Chicago softball player in *About Last Night* . . .** (1986), **and a star member of the crew team in *Oxford Blues*** (1984)

Al Pacino as an auto racer in *Bobby Deerfield* (1977)

Kip Pardue as a prep football star named Sunshine in *Remember the Titans* (2000)

Anthony Perkins as mentally troubled baseball player Jimmy Piersall in *Fear Strikes Out* (1957) and as a basketball player in *Tall Story* (1960)

Keanu Reeves as a former college quarterback in *Point Break* (1991) and in *The Replacements* (2000)

Tim Robbins as minor league pitching phenom Nuke LaLoosh in *Bull Durham* (1988)

Adam Sandler as a college linebacker in *The Waterboy* (1998)

10
documentaries
that are
better
than most
feature
films

10 documentaries that are better than most feature films

American Movie (1999)

Affectionate look at a well-intentioned but marginally talented Wisconsin handyman who makes incredibly terrible movies in his backyard, using friends and relatives as actors.

Devil's Playground (2002)

When Amish children turn 16, they're allowed to explore the "English world," which means they smoke, drink, do drugs, have sex, and get into rock and roll. Lucy Walker's amazing documentary follows a group of Amish teenagers as they indulge their modern-world fantasies and then decide whether to return to the Amish way of life.

The Endurance: Shackleton's Legendary Antarctic Expedition (2000)

You know those rich guys who are always trying to set world records for flying around the world in a balloon, or climbing the highest peaks on seven continents? They're wimps compared to Ernest Shackleton, whose failed attempt to cross the Antarctic landmass in 1914 resulted in a 22-month struggle to survive in conditions that were beyond brutal.

Go Tigers! (2001)

In football-crazed Massillon, Ohio, the prep gridiron heroes are treated like gods while the rest of the school system struggles to stay above water.

Hearts of Darkness: A Filmmaker's Apocalypse (1991)

Fascinating documentary about the off-screen madness that accompanied the making of Apocalypse Now.

Home Movie (2001)

Director Chris Smith, who also did American Movie, takes us inside some of the strangest homes in the United States, including a treehouse in the Hawaiian rain forest and an entire dwelling built in a former missile silo, with walls and ceilings thick enough to withstand a nuclear attack.

Hoop Dreams (1994)

One of the best documentaries ever made, it covers six years in the lives of two Chicago prep basketball stars who dream of making it in the NBA.

The Kid Stays in the Picture (2002)

Adaptation of the cult hit autobiography of Robert Evans, the legendary producer who went from clothier to actor to studio chief and was partially responsible for such movies as Love Story, Rosemary's Baby, and The Godfather.

Mr. Death: The Rise and Fall of Fred A. Leuchter, Jr. (1999)

Astonishing and heartwrenching look at a bizarre man who perfected the electric chair and became a staunch believer in the crackpot theory that the Holocaust never took place.

Startup.com (2001)

The meteoric rise and spectacular fall of a dotcom project as experienced by two longtime friends.

most
critics
loved
it!
I didn't!

most critics loved it! I didn't!

 n the order of the amount of hate mail my thumbs-down vote generated, here are 15 acclaimed films of the last few years that just didn't do it for me:

1. **The Lord of the Rings: The Fellowship of the Ring** (2001)*
2. **Chicken Run** (2000)
3. **Hedwig and the Angry Inch** (2001)
4. **O Brother, Where Art Thou?** (2000)
5. **Spy Kids** (2001)
6. **Metropolis** (2001)
7. **Girlfight** (2000)
8. **Chuck & Buck** (2000)
9. **Nurse Betty** (2000)
10. **The Widow of St. Pierre** (2000)
11. **The Piano Teacher** (2001)
12. **The Lady and the Duke** (2001)
13. **Enigma** (2001)
14. **The House of Mirth** (2000)
15. **In the Mood for Love** (2001)

Note: The volume of calls, letters, faxes, and e-mails I received about Lord of the Rings was greater than the total amount of responses to the other 14 films on this list.

panned
by many,
enjoyed
by me

panned by many, enjoyed by me

hese films were ripped by most critics—and I have to admit it appears to be a frightening list at first glance. Still, I gave each of these movies a thumbs-up, and I stand by my thumb, which is something you usually don't see outside of a John Woo film.

3000 Miles to Graceland (2001)

Angel Eyes (2001)

Book of Shadows: Blair Witch 2 (2000)

The Cell (2001)

Coyote Ugly (2000)

Final Fantasy: The Spirits Within (2001)

Josie and the Pussycats (2001)

A Knight's Tale (2001)

Life or Something Like It (2002)

Not Another Teen Movie (2002)

Planet of the Apes (2001)

Reign of Fire (2002)

Rock Star (2001)

Star Wars: Episode II—Attack of the Clones (2002)

Stolen Summer (2002)

Swordfish (2001)

What Planet Are You From? (2000)

making
a
scene

making a scene

 hoice excerpts from some of my favorite monologues from
the last 25 years . . .

Steve Martin in Planes, Trains & Automobiles *(1987)*

*Forced to share a crummy hotel room with the unbearably
cheerful Del Griffith, played by the late great John Candy, Martin's
Neal finally lets loose with his true feelings:*

"And by the way, you know, when you're telling these little stories,
here's a good idea: have a point. It makes it so much more interesting for the listener!"

Julia Roberts in Erin Brockovich *(2000)*

*The biker next door asks Erin for her phone number—and gets
more than he bargained for:*

"How about this for a number, six. That's how old my other daughter
is. Eight is the age of my son. Two is how many times I've been married and divorced. Sixteen is the number of dollars I have in my bank
account. 850-3943. That's my phone number, and with all the numbers I gave you, I'm guessing zero is the number of times you're going
to call it."

Bill Murray in Caddyshack (1980)

In perhaps the most-quoted guy monologue of modern times, greenskeeper Carl Spackler keeps a pitchfork pressed against the neck of a silent, petrified kid and tells the story of the time he caddied for the Dalai Lama:

"So we finish the 18th and he's gonna stiff me! And I say, 'Hey, Lama, hey, how about a little something, you know, for the effort, you know?' And he says, 'Oh, uh, there won't be any money, but when you die, on your deathbed, you will receive total consciousness.' So I got that goin' for me, which is nice."

Philip Seymour Hoffman in Almost Famous (2000)

Legendary rock critic Lester Bangs tries to dampen the dreams of William, a bright-eyed teenager and aspiring music writer:

"I'm telling you, you're coming along at a very dangerous time for rock and roll. And that's why I think you should just turn around, go back, you know, and be a lawyer or something. But I can tell from your face that you won't. I can give you thirty-five bucks. Give me a thousand words on Black Sabbath."

Steve Buscemi in Reservoir Dogs (1992)

Having just analyzed the real meaning of Madonna's "Like a Virgin," the gang of thieves, who know each other only by color-coded names, is about to exit a diner—but Mr. Pink, played by Steve Buscemi, has refused to "throw in a buck" for the tip. He explains why:

"And as for this non-college bullshit I got two words for that: learn to fuckin' type, 'cause if you're expecting me to help out with the rent you're in for a big fuckin' surprise."

making a scene

Jack Nicholson in A Few Good Men (1992)

Testifying in the court-martial trial of two of his men who are accused of killing a soldier during an illegal "code red" hazing, Nicholson's hardcore Col. Nathan Jessep blows up on the stand:

"We use words like honor, code, loyalty. We use these words as the backbone of a life spent defending something. You use them as a punchline. I have neither the time nor the inclination to explain myself to a man who rises and sleeps under the blanket of the very freedom that I provide and then questions the manner in which I provide it."

worst
ethnic
casting

worst ethnic casting

although some Mexicans believed the American-born Latina Jennifer Lopez shouldn't have been cast in the role of the slain pop singer Selena, and a number of Brits were appalled when Texas gal Renée Zellweger nabbed the plum title role in *Bridget Jones's Diary*, both actresses were so good that they transcended the differences between their own heritage and that of the characters they played. It would be ludicrous to argue that every ethnic role must be awarded to someone with the exact heritage as the character. Was Ben Kingsley not effective as Gandhi? Didn't Olivier handle Othello?

But there are limits. Consider these disastrous casting decisions:

Wallace Beery as Pancho Villa in *Viva Villa!* (1934)

Spencer Tracy and John Garfield as Mexicans in *Tortilla Flat* (1942)

John Wayne as Genghis Khan in *The Conqueror* (1956)

Marlon Brando as a native of Okinawa in *The Teahouse of the August Moon* (1956)

Victor Mature in the title role in *Chief Crazy Horse* (1955)

Frank Sinatra as a Spanish guerrilla in *The Pride and the Passion* (1957)

Charlton Heston as a Mexican in *A Touch of Evil* (1958)

Edward G. Robinson giving rise to a million "Where's your God now, where's your Moses NOW!" imitations as Dathan in *The Ten Commandments* (1956)

Natalie Wood as a Puerto Rican–American in *West Side Story* (1961)

Paul Muni as a Chinese man in *The Good Earth* (1937)

Katharine Hepburn as a Chinese woman in *Dragon Seed* (1944)

And most egregious of all, Mickey Rooney as a buck-toothed Japanese man with Coke-bottle glasses in *Breakfast at Tiffany's* (1961)

the 10 highly stupid habits of movie people

the 10 highly stupid habits of movie people

1. When the hero has the bad guy trapped in a warehouse or an abandoned mansion on a hill and the bad guy runs upstairs or into a dark room, the hero always runs after the bad guy, instead of going outside and calling for backup.

2. Upon shooting the bad guy, the hero will holster his gun and walk up to the bad guy to make sure the bad guy is really dead. Just as he's about to touch the bad guy, the bad guy will spring into action and start throttling the hero until he's shot about six more times.

3. When the hero is being choked by the bad guy, he or she always tries to yank the bad guy's hands away—instead of just bending back one finger.

4. Characters who are too distraught to obey the basic rules of traffic will cross against the light, putting their hands up to halt cars and ducking out of the way as horns blare and tires squeal and drivers shout things like, "Why don't you watch where you're going!" and "Are you crazy? You're going to get killed!"

5. When someone hangs up the phone in the movies, the person on the other end of the line always says, "Hello? Hello? Hello?" at least three times and then looks at the phone and

says "Hello?" at least once more before reaching the obvious conclusion that the other person has hung up.

6. When a car won't start, movie people will repeatedly turn the ignition and pump the accelerator pedal while saying, "Come on!" over and over. (Then again, this technique, which usually results in a flooded engine in real life, often works in movies, so maybe it's not so stupid after all.)

7. All strange, frightening, and potentially life-threatening disturbances in the house should be immediately investigated, even if that means a character will be walking into a dark room in her nightgown without a weapon.

8. If the lead in a romantic comedy overhears a conversation that makes it seem like the person she's in love with is having an affair, she will cut off all communication with the guy rather than confronting him—lest he clear up the whole misunderstanding in five minutes and bring the entire movie to a halt.

9. When pursuing the bad guys or fleeing danger, the good guy will punch an elevator button several times in rapid succession, curse at the elevator—and then head for the stairwell, even if it means a forty-story climb.

10. Rather than investigating claims of impending danger, security guards and cops in the movies always laugh off the report, which usually means they'll be dead within minutes.

12 reasons why I'll never attend a Freddie Prinze, Jr., film festival

12 reasons why I'll never attend a Freddie Prinze, Jr., film festival

Scooby-Doo (2002)

Summer Catch (2001)

Head Over Heels (2001)

Boys and Girls (2000)

Down to You (2000)

Wing Commander (1999)

She's All That (1999)

Vig (1998)

I Still Know What You Did Last Summer (1998)*

I Know What You Did Last Summer (1997)

The House of Yes (1997)

To Gillian on Her 37th Birthday (1996)

*Seeing as how I Still Know What You Did Last Summer *picks up a year AFTER* I Know What You Did Last Summer, *shouldn't the title be* I Still Know What You Did Two Years Ago?

actors-
in-
chief

actors-in-chief

 ased on the quality of the performance and the strength of the character, my picks for the greatest fictional presidents:

1. Harrison Ford in *Air Force One* (1997)

Apparently those Russian terrorists who hijacked the president's plane didn't realize the guy was Han Solo and Indiana Jones rolled into one!

2. Bill Pullman in *Independence Day* (1996)

Even though entire metropolitan areas have been decimated by alien invaders and his wife is toast, the fighter pilot–turned-prez climbs into a jet and leads the charge against those gooey aliens. You gotta figure his approval rating soared after that.

3. Morgan Freeman in *Deep Impact* (1998)

A comet "the size of Mt. Everest" is hurtling toward earth, so Freeman approves a joint U.S.-Soviet mission to intercept the comet and explode it with nuclear devices. And because he's calm, steady, reassuring Morgan Freeman, we think: Good plan!

4. Michael Douglas in *The American President* (1995)

As President Andrew Shepherd, a widower with a young daughter, Douglas is facing a tough re-election campaign against a vicious right-wing senator played by Richard Dreyfuss. Unlike the above heroes, President Shepherd doesn't thwart a hijacking, maintain global calm during a worldwide catastrophe, or beat back an army of alien invaders—but he does win the heart of Annette Bening.

5. Jeff Bridges in *The Contender* (2000)

Like the Douglas character in The American President, *Bridges is given a name that sounds presidential: He's Jackson Evans, a liberal president nearing the end of his second term who taps Senator Laine Hanson, played by Joan Allen, to succeed the recently deceased vice president. Even when it appears certain that a scandal will doom Allen's chances and taint his own legacy, President Evans stands by his man—I mean, woman—and systematically eliminates his enemies. When Evans orders up a shark sandwich from the White House kitchen, it's as if he's eating one of his own.*

6. Kevin Kline in *Dave* (1993)

Kline plays the kind of part Alec Guinness would have taken 40 years earlier: a dual role as cold-blooded President Bill Mitchell and warmhearted Dave Kovic, an idealistic social activist who looks exactly like the president and is pressed into what is supposed to be ceremonial duty when the president is felled by a stroke. Not only does "President" Dave repair the budget, restore social programs, and arrange it so that his noble vice president (played by Ben Kingsley) will become his successor, he also beds First Lady Sigourney Weaver. And to think most celebrity lookalikes just get a few hundred bucks for appearing at store openings and radio station promotional events.

impeachable

presidents

impeachable presidents

rom the worst to the only somewhat horrible, these are the lousiest, scariest, most corrupt fictional movie presidents:

1. Gene Hackman in *Absolute Power* (1997)

President Allen Richmond is a rotten, soulless, corrupt philanderer who murders his mistress (who was married to his lifelong mentor).

2. Michael Belson in *Wag the Dog* (1997)

It's a minor role, but the reason the main characters in this film essentially invent a war is to distract the public from a brewing scandal after the president gets mixed up with an underage "Firefly Girl" right in the Oval Office. (Apparently the Girl Scouts of America weren't too keen on lending their good name to this movie.)

3. John Travolta in *Primary Colors* (1998)

True, Travolta's lusty, corrupt, doughnut-chomping, Clintonian character is a candidate and not the president through most of the film, but in the final shot we see him dancing with his wife after his inauguration. And we just know that President Jack Stanton is destined to rendezvous with a Firefly Girl in the Oval Office someday.

4. Donald Moffat in *Clear and Present Danger* (1994)

Moffat's President Edward Bennett (there's another one of those generically presidential-sounding names) is a weak puppet.

5. Jack Nicholson in *Mars Attacks!* (1996)

Nicholson's President James Dale is a boorish, unfunny dimwit in the most expensive B movie ever made.

6. Anthony Hopkins in *Nixon* (1995)

Hopkins sweats, drinks, and swears up a storm as the title character in Oliver Stone's highly fictionalized portrayal of Richard M. Nixon.

10 movie character imitations that **men** can't **resist** doing

10 movie character imitations that men can't resist doing

a s a social experiment, find any man between the ages of 15 and 45 and ask him if he can do any or all of the following imitations.

That's the easy part. Now try getting him to stop.

1. Bill Murray's "It's in the hole!" routine from *Caddyshack.*

2. Clint Eastwood as Dirty Harry: "I know what you're thinking. Did he fire six shots or only five? Well, to tell you the truth, in all this excitement, I've kinda lost track myself."

3. Jimmy Stewart in *It's a Wonderful Life,* running through the streets of Bedford Falls: "Merry Christmas, you old lamppost!"

4. Vince Vaughn in *Swingers,* telling John Favreau he's got the goods: "You are so money, baby!"

5. Austin Powers: "Do I make you horny, baby?"

6. Dr. Evil: "I'm prepared to offer you . . . one MILLION dollars."

7. John Wayne, Jimmy Cagney, Humphrey Bogart, and Cary Grant. (Actually, we don't do imitations of these old-time stars. We do imitations of guys like Rich Little doing imitations.)

8. Arnold Schwarzenegger in *The Terminator,* telling the cops, "I'll be back."

9. Sylvester Stallone in *Rocky.*

10. John Travolta and Samuel L. Jackson in *Pulp Fiction,* discussing the difference between the United States and Europe: "You know what they call a Quarter Pounder with Cheese in Paris? . . . A 'Royale' with Cheese."

imitations
women
just **can't**
resist
doing

imitations women just can't resist doing

Women don't do imitations. Come on—when was the last time you heard a woman say, "Have you ever heard my impression of Meg Ryan in *You've Got Mail*?" Doesn't happen!

friends
shouldn't
let
friends

make

movies

friends shouldn't let friends make movies

he six core members of *Friends* are all talented, attractive, and EXTREMELY LUCKY actors who have earned tens of millions of dollars and have become household names as a result of their work on the popular NBC sitcom. But as film actors, they have a lot more strikeouts than home runs:

Jennifer Aniston

Leprechaun (1993)

She's the One (1996)

Picture Perfect (1997)

Dream for an Insomniac (1998)

Courteney Cox Arquette

Masters of the Universe (1987)

Sketch Artist II: Hands That See (1995)

The Shrink Is In (2000)

Lisa Kudrow

The Crazysitter (1995)

Hacks (1997)

Clockwatchers (1997)

Hanging Up (2000)

Lucky Numbers (2000)

Matt LeBlanc

Ed (1996)

Lost in Space (1998)

Charlie's Angels (2000)

Matthew Perry

Fools Rush In (1997)

Almost Heroes (1998)

Three to Tango (1999)

David Schwimmer

Kissing a Fool (1998)

Six Days Seven Nights (1998)

All the Rage (1999)

Love & Sex (2000)

7 good
movies
featuring **one**
of the
"friends"

7 good movies featuring one of the "friends"

Apt Pupil (1998) — David Schwimmer

The Good Girl (2002) — Jennifer Aniston

Office Space (1999) — Jennifer Aniston

The Opposite of Sex (1998) — Lisa Kudrow

The Whole Nine Yards (2000) — Matthew Perry

Romy and Michele's High School Reunion (1997) — Lisa Kudrow

Scream (1996) — Courteney Cox Arquette

Note: Matt LeBlanc has yet to appear in a good movie. But I'm sure he's a nice guy.

the gross-out hall of fame

the gross-out hall of fame

maggots, feces, and scrotum. No, that's not the name of a one-hit wonder trio from the 1960s, it's the unholy trio of elements most often utilized in lamebrain comedies and gut-churning horror flicks. Food and drink are allowed in the screening room in Chicago where I watch about a half-dozen movies per week, and these screenings often take place around lunchtime—but one must be careful not to be biting into a meatball sandwich when a Tom Green "comedy" is playing. Talk about an appetite killer. The most disgusting gross-out moments from films of the last few years:

Austin Powers in Goldmember (2002)

A very funny movie—but also an extremely disgusting one, with Goldmember eating flakes of his own peeling skin; Fred Wonder Years *Savage as a mole who has a giant mole on his face; Fat Bastard waxing philosophical about his flatulence and his feces; and multiple urination jokes.*

Hannibal (2001)

Anthony Hopkins prepares a piece of Ray Liotta's brain and then serves it to the still-conscious Liotta, who eats it at the dinner table while sporting a screw-top cranium.

National Lampoon's Van Wilder (2002)

A bulldog with enormously oversized scrotum is "milked" and produces enough sperm to fill a box of éclairs, which are sent to a fraternity as a prank. If that's not enough, we get a prolonged scene of the frat boys scarfing down the gooey pastries as the "cream" runs down their faces.

Freddy Got Fingered (2001)

The aforementioned Mr. Green delivers a baby, swings it around by its umbilical cord, and then chews on the cord, in an obvious nod to the works of Noel Coward. Green also manually stimulates a horse. (Apparently bestiality is a favorite theme among humor-impaired screenwriters.) And Rip Torn, playing Green's father, wiggles his naked rear end at Green and invites him to . . . well.

Monkeybone (2001)

Brendan Fraser's Stu temporarily occupies the corpse of a recently deceased gymnast played by Chris Kattan (don't ask), whose organs burst from his body, fall from the sky (again, don't ask), and land on people's heads and on a barbecue grill (please don't ask).

Saving Silverman (2001)

We're treated to a graphic scene of silicone implants being inserted into the buttocks of Jason Biggs, best known for boinking a homemade dessert in American Pie. (Can't wait for his American Film Institute tribute!) There's also a scene of a high school football coach, played by R. Lee Ermey of Full Metal Jacket fame, defecating on a front lawn. Just when you think the camera will pull away, it doesn't.

Say It Isn't So (2001)

Chris Klein—another American Pie alum—walks down a street with his arm jammed up a cow's ass. Two-time Academy Award–

the gross-out hall of fame

winner Sally Field plays Klein's mother, and has a showcase scene in which she adds "salt" to a sandwich by rubbing it under her arms.

See Spot Run (2001)

Paul Sorvino loses his testicles to dog attacks—IN SEPARATE INCIDENTS. David Arquette stars as a loser mailman who at one point is nearly covered in feces. That pretty much sums up how we feel watching this movie.

Tomcats (2001)

In yet another variation on the losing-a-testicle theme, Jake Busey forfeits a testicle to cancer and makes Jerry O'Connell promise he'll retrieve it from the hospital lab. O'Connell succeeds in locating the organ, but it slips from his grasp and bounces around the hospital like a SuperBall until it finally comes to rest on the lunch plate of the physician who removed it. The doctor then eats it.

Bones (2001)

I actually enjoyed this campy blaxploitation horror farce starring Snoop Dogg as a hustler/pimp from the 1970s who comes back from the dead to torment his betrayers—but it took me days to recover from the scene where a rabid, possessed dog projectile-vomits thousands of maggots onto the faces and bodies of several people.

The Sweetest Thing (2002)

Speaking of maggots—and I sincerely hope this will be the last time I do so in this or any other book—there's a scene in this dreadful romantic comedy in which Cameron Diaz and Christina Applegate find an ancient piece of meat, wrapped in aluminum foil shaped like a bird, and fling it out of their car. The foil-bird takes flight like an eagle, only to swoop around and land smack on the windshield of the car, whereupon it explodes and maggots fly everywhere. This leads to a scene where Diaz and Applegate sneak into the men's room at a gas station to clean up, whereupon they're victimized by an exploding urinal.

Incredibly, The Sweetest Thing received no Academy Award nominations.*

*Note: I wrote this months before the 2002 Oscar nominations were announced in February of 2003, but if The Sweetest Thing gets any nominations, I will donate all of my royalties from the proceeds of this book to People for the Ethical Treatment of Animals, with instructions that the money be used to preserve the maggot.

attack
of the
quote
whores

attack of the quote whores

he movies were bad, but the quotes were classics!

"Tremendously funny. The surprise comedy of the year!"—Shawn Edwards of WDAF-TV, on *Black Knight*

"*Battlefield Earth* will rock America!"—Maria Salas, Telemundo/Gems TV, on *Battlefield Earth*

"Feverishly funny!"—Steve Iervolino, Launch, on *Osmosis Jones*

"The first great film of 2001."—Jeff Craig, Sixty Second Preview, on *15 Minutes*

"Inspired insanity!"—Mark S. Allen, KMAX-TV, on *Freddy Got Fingered*

"May be the best date movie ever!"—Bill Bregoli, Westwood One, on *Keeping the Faith*

"Heartwarming! Hysterical! The perfect family film!"—Jim Svejda, KNX/CBS Radio, on *Jungle 2 Jungle*

"One of the summer's best!"—Joel Siegel, *Good Morning America*, on *Striptease*

"This movie kicks major butt!"—Jeff Craig, Sixty Second Preview, on *Tank Girl*

"It's the year's first happy surprise! Fun at full tilt...A wow cast."—Peter Travers, *Rolling Stone,* on *Orange County*

"You'll have no trouble laughing big!"—Jeanne Wolf, on *Big Trouble*

"A funny, feel-good 10! You'll have a smile on your face and a tear in your eye at this happy, heart-warming family comedy that's heaven-sent for the holiday season."—Susan Granger, AMC, on *Dear God*

"A hilarious comic action *Odd Couple.* Lots of laughs, along with some heart-stopping action."—Jeanne Wolf, on *Showtime*

"Riveting!"—Jim Ferguson, Prevue Channel, on *The Juror*

"A sexy, fresh and wildly hip comedy! The makers of *Bridget Jones's Diary* and *Notting Hill* have done it again!"—Earl Dittman, on *40 Days and 40 Nights*

"The most powerful film of the decade."—Maria Salas, Tele-mundo/Gems, on *187*

"Hilarious! Robin and Edward are sensational."—Jim Ferguson, KMSB-TV, on *Death to Smoochy*

attack of the quote whores

"*Animal House* meets *Some Like It Hot.*"—Dennis Harvey, *Daily Variety*, on *Sorority Boys*

"A *Back to the Future* for a new generation."—Paul Saucido, LATV Live, on *Clockstoppers*

"Nonstop fun!"—Jim Ferguson, then of the Prevue Channel, on *She's the One*

"I laughed, I cried, and, the most magical feeling of all, I glowed while watching."—Thelma Adams, *New York Post*, on *The Secret of Roan Inish*. (She glowed? Quick, call the Nuclear Regulatory Commission!)

"The most terrifying film of the decade."—Maria Salas, Telemundo/Gems TV, on *Deep Blue Sea*

"Amazing and unforgettable."—Jeff Craig, Sixty Second Preview, on *Murder in the First*

"One of the best films of the decade!"—Sara Edwards, NBC-TV on *Anna and the King*

"Simply out of this world!"—Ron Brewington, American Urban Radio Networks, on *Lost in Space*

"An action-packed, rip-roaring adventure."—Bonnie Churchill, the National News Syndicate, on *The Newton Boys*

"Great laughs! Great performances! The most fun film in decades!" —Barry ZeVan, Channel America, on *The Beverly Hillbillies*

"The most beautiful movie of the millennium."—David Sheehan, CBS-TV, on *Bicentennial Man*

"One of the best pictures of the year!"—Cary Burglund, KCAL, on *Crazy in Alabama*

"It's invigorating and warmhearted. Say five 'Hail Whoopis!' and see it!"—Ralph Novak, *People* magazine, on *Sister Act 2*

"A 10. Really, a 13."—Gary Franklin, KCOP-Channel 13, on *The Joy Luck Club* (Note: I liked *The Joy Luck Club*. I just don't understand how a movie can get a 13 on a scale of 1–10. It's like the amplifier in *Spiñal Tap* that goes to 11.)

"I laughed, I cried, I spun the emotional wheel!"—Geri Richter Campbell, *Jane* magazine, on *Hope Floats*

"You never had so much fun at the movies and probably never will."—Bonnie Churchill, National News Syndicate, on *Tank Girl* (Hey. If *Tank Girl* were the most fun I could ever have at the movies, I'd stop going to the movies.)

always
after me
lucky
charms!

(actors who have *tried* to do Irish accents)

always after me lucky charms!
(actors who have *tried* to do Irish accents)

On a scale of 1 to 10, with 10 being the best:

Liam Neeson in *Michael Collins* (1996)—10*

Sean Connery in *The Untouchables* (1987)—9

Robert Mitchum in *Ryan's Daughter* (1970)—8

James Cromwell in *L.A. Confidential* (1997)—8

Robin Wright Penn in *The Playboys* (1992)—7

Johnny Depp in *Chocolat* (2000)—7

Kate Hudson in *About Adam* (2000)—5

Brad Pitt in *The Devil's Own* (1997)—5

Ryan O'Neal in *Barry Lyndon* (1975)—5

Tom Cruise in *Far and Away* (1992)—4

Julia Roberts in *Mary Reilly* (1996)—4

Julia Roberts in *Michael Collins* (1996)—3

Richard Gere in *The Jackal* (1997)—2

Mickey Rourke in *A Prayer for the Dying* (1987)—2

Note: Neeson is Irish. I suppose that gives him something of an advantage.

let
me
guess,
your
number
starts with
"555"

let me guess, your number starts with "555"

f a movie character has to make a phone call, odds are the number will be a phony with a 555-prefix—the thought being that if a real number were used, thousands of bored losers would dial it and harass some poor schlub whose private home line is in the latest Adam Sandler movie. (Not that they'd run out of the theater, but with movies playing forever on cable and DVD, it's the home viewer/loser you have to worry about.) With a few exceptions that have fun with the cliché, such as *Magnolia* and *Last Action Hero,* films continue to take us out of the story by using the 555-number, which always screams, "You're watching a movie! None of this is real!"

Here are some of the 555-numbers of some famous movie characters. Warning: A lot of these people have Caller ID, so if you dial the number and hang up, they'll know it's you.

Lester Burnham (Kevin Spacey) in *American Beauty*: 555-0199

Nick Marshall (Mel Gibson) in *What Women Want:* 555-1226

Lloyd Dobler (John Cusack) in *Say Anything . . .*: 555-1342

Joel Goodson (Tom Cruise) in *Risky Business:* 555-2121

Lana (Rebecca De Mornay) in *Risky Business:* 555-3365

SanDeE* (Sarah Jessica Parker, and yeah, her character spelled it that way) in *L.A. Story:* 555-2312

Chip Douglas (Jim Carrey) in *The Cable Guy:* 555-4329

Dan Gallagher (Michael Douglas) in *Fatal Attraction:* 555-8129

"Doc" Brown (Christopher Lloyd) in *Back to the Future:* 555-4385

The limo guy's cell phone number in *Die Hard:* 555-3213

The Jarrett household in *Ordinary People:* 555-2368

The *Ghostbusters* hot line: 555-2368

Monster Joe's in *Pulp Fiction:* 555-7908; 555-7909

The French military in *Godzilla:* 555-7600

Mr. Pizza Guy in *Fast Times at Ridgemont High:* 555-8216

Listener line in *Talk Radio:* 555-TALK

Morrie's Wigs in *GoodFellas:* 555-HAIR

Note: Certain license plate numbers are also used again and again in films, for the same reasons the 555-prefix is often used. Probably the most common California license plate number in films is 2GAT123, which has appeared in Traffic, Mulholland Dr., crazy/beautiful, Beverly Hills Cop 2, Pay It Forward, *and* L.A. Story, *to name just a few. Watch for it.*

annie
name
will **do**

annie name will do

n addition to the little orphan named Annie and Annie Oakley and of course Annie Hall, there have been dozens of other movie characters named Annie. (Even young Anakin Skywalker is called "Annie" in *The Phantom Menace* and *Attack of the Clones*.) If your leading lady is supposed to be plucky, smart, and cute as a button, call her Annie! Susan Sarandon in *Bull Durham*, Meg Ryan in *Sleepless in Seattle*, Kimberly Williams in *Father of the Bride*, Sandra Bullock in *Speed*—Annies one and all. In fact there's been a virtual epidemic of Annies in the last few decades:

Jennifer Aniston—Annie Hughes in *The Iron Giant* (1999)

Anne Archer—Annie in *Paradise Alley* (1978)

Kerry Armstrong—Annie in *Grievous Bodily Harm* (1988)

Jayne Atkinson—Annie Greenwood in *Free Willy* (1993)

Cate Blanchett—Annie Wilson in *The Gift* (2000)

Lois Chiles—Annie Lansing in *Creepshow 2* (1987)

Denise Faye—Annie in *Chicago: The Musical* (2002)

Heather Graham—Annie in *Sidewalks of New York* (2001)

Mary Gross—Annie Herman in *Troop Beverly Hills* (1989)

Carla Gugino—Annie in *The Jimmy Show* (2002)

Goldie Hawn—Annie in *Overboard* (1987)

Helen Hunt—Annie in *Mr. Saturday Night* (1992)

Diane Keaton—Annie in *Annie Hall* (1977)

Diane Keaton—Annie MacDuggan Paradis in *The First Wives Club* (1996)

Moira Kelly—Annie Hawks in *Unhook the Stars* (1996)

Jo Kendall—Annie in *Howards End* (1992)

Jennifer Jason Leigh—Annie Sullivan in *Road to Perdition* (2002)

Emily Lloyd—Annie McGee in *Welcome to Sarajevo* (1997)

Amy Madigan—Anni Kinsella in *Field of Dreams* (1989)

Janet May—Annie in *Crossroads* (2002)

Kelly McGillis—Annie in *Made in Heaven* (1987)

Julia McNeal—Annie in *Urban Legend* (1994)

Robbi Morgan—Annie in *Friday the 13th* (1980)

Larissa Murray—Annie in *Don't Look Back!* (2001)

Lisa Parker—Annie in *Bar Girls* (1994)

Sarah Paulson—Annie in *What Women Want* (2000)

Aileen Quinn—Annie in *Annie* (1982)

Annie Rusoff—Annie in *Pump Up the Volume* (1990)

Meg Ryan—Annie Reed in *Sleepless in Seattle* (1993)

Susan Sarandon—Annie Savoy in *Bull Durham* (1998)

Annabella Sciorra—Annie Nielsen in *What Dreams May Come* (1998)

Kristin Scott Thomas—Annie MacLean in *The Horse Whisperer* (1998)

Ally Sheedy—Annie in *Blue City* (1986)

Elisabeth Shue—Annie in *The Trigger Effect* (1996)

Robin Tunney—Annie Garrett in *Vertical Limit* (2000)

Tracy Vilar—Annie in *Grace of my Heart* (1996)

Lynette Walden—Annie in *Corrina, Corrina* (1994)

Diane Weist—Annie in *I Am Sam* (2001)

Julie Whitney—Annie in *Eight Men Out* (1988)

annie name will do

Kimberly Williams—Annie in *Father of the Bride* (1991)

Michelle Williams—Annie in *Timemaster* (1995)

Sean Young—Annie in *The Invader* (1997)

good will

will

recycling

good will recycling

en Affleck and Matt Damon won the Academy Award for Best Screenplay for *Good Will Hunting*—but not every idea in the script was original. The screenplay borrows from not one, not two, but three popular urban legends—stories that seem too good to be true because they ARE too good to be true.

1. The setup of the movie is based on the urban legend about a mathematics professor who keeps an "unsolvable" equation chalked on the blackboard in his classroom—until an unwitting freshman walks in one day and promptly answers the question correctly, proving that he's a genius of the highest order. In *Good Will Hunting*, Damon plays a janitor who solves a series of difficult equations posted on the blackboard by a snooty professor.

2. The second urban legend is repackaged as a "true story" told by one of Will's townie friends, Chuckie. According to Chuckie, his uncle Marty was on his way home after a heavy night of drinking when he was pulled over by a cop. Just as the cop began administering a sobriety test, another car zoomed past and crashed into a tree about 50 yards down the road.

   "Stay put!" the cop told Marty before running to the scene of the accident.

   But Marty jumped into the car, drove home, put the car in the garage, and told his wife, "If anyone should ask, say I was home with you and the kids all night."

The next morning, the policeman came to Marty's door and said, "You took off on me last night."

Marty denied everything, but the cop asked to see Marty's car. They opened the garage door—and there was the policeman's car.

Funny how that happened to Chuckie, because it's been a popular urban legend for decades.

3. The third urban legend in *Good Will Hunting* is recycled as a joke Will tells to his therapist, played by Robin Williams. It's the old story about a pilot who accidentally leaves the intercom on as he muses, "I sure could go for a cup of coffee and some [oral sex.]" When a flight attendant goes rushing up the aisle to tell the pilot he's left the microphone on, a passenger hollers, "You forgot the coffee, honey!"

The published screenplay contains yet another urban legend— the old story about the guy who mistakenly thinks he has struck and killed the neighbor's cat with his car, and decides to put the limping cat out of its misery, only to learn, too late, that it was another cat he had struck with the car. But this scene didn't make it into the film.

Not that *Good Will Hunting* is the only film to dip into the world of urban legends for story material. For example, *Magnolia* begins with a series of vignettes that are all based on urban legends. But using these stories isn't plagiarism because urban legends are modern folktales, created by an anonymous committee of storytellers who don't even know each other. Nobody ever steps forward to claim authorship of these stories. Even if a writer wanted to ask permission, there's nobody to ask.

5 reasons why George Bailey isn't such a wonderful guy in *It's a Wonderful Life*

5 reasons why George Bailey isn't such a wonderful guy in *It's a Wonderful Life*

'm not disputing that *It's a Wonderful Life* is an American classic—though I prefer *Miracle on 34th Street* as the quintessential Christmas movie—but if one dissects the plot points, the argument can be made that George Bailey is kind of a jerk under pressure, wonderful life or not.

1. When George learns that Uncle Billy has lost the $8,000, he roughs up the kindly, absentminded old fellow, grabbing him by the lapels (that's assault and battery right there) and screaming, "Where's that money you silly stupid old fool? Where's that money? Do you realize what this means? It means bankruptcy and scandal and prison. That's what it means. One of us is going to jail—well it's not gonna be me!"

   Great. The guy's going to sell his own uncle down the river for a perfectly innocent mistake.

2. After the money is lost, George goes home and terrorizes the entire family without explanation. When dear sweet Mary asks what's wrong, he bellows, "Everything's wrong! You call this a happy family? Why did we have to have all these kids?"

   Some family man. The first sign of financial crisis and he's lamenting the births of his children!

3. Continuing his streak of verbal abuse, George berates Zuzu's teacher over the phone, calling her "stupid, silly [and] careless."

4. When Mary asks, "George, must you torture the children, too?" his response is to run out of the house and head for the nearest bar, Martini's, where he behaves rudely and slugs down drink after drink before getting punched by Zuzu's teacher's husband and staggering out of the bar and into his car.

   I smell a DUI!

5. Sure enough, the inebriated George forgets to turn on his headlights and is soon swerving through the streets of Bedford Falls before crashing into a tree. And what does this drunk driver do when the homeowner comes running out to see a car on the front lawn? He leaves the scene of the accident.

   So when the story comes to its happy ending and George says, "Attaboy, Clarence" while the townsfolk sing "Auld Lang Syne," consider George's life after the movie. He'll have to take up another collection to cover his legal expenses on charges of driving under the influence, improper lane usage, reckless driving, criminal damage to property, and leaving the scene of an accident.

   I guess Mr. Potter put it best when he said, "And a Happy New Year to you—in jail!"

movies
that
never
played
on an
airplane

movies that never played on an airplane

Air Force One—Harrison Ford is the president and Gary Oldman is the terrorist who takes over his plane.

Airplane!—Spoof of the *Airport* movies.

Airport—First of the big airplane-disaster films.

Alive—After a rugby team's plane crashes in the Andes, survivors have to resort to eating their dead friends.

Bounce—As snow blankets O'Hare Airport, Ben Affleck gives up his seat to married guy Tony Goldwyn so Affleck can score with Natasha Henstridge. The plane crashes, killing everyone on board.

Cast Away—Tom Hanks is the lone survivor when a FedEx plane is felled by a storm.

Die Hard 2—Terrorists sabotage the air control tower at the airport in Denver and intentionally crash a plane, killing everyone on board, despite the heroic efforts of Bruce Willis's John McClane.

Fearless—Jeff Bridges deals with feelings of guilt and alienation after being one of the few survivors of a plane crash.

Final Destination—When a high school student has a premonition that his plane is going to crash, he causes a disturbance that results in several of the students and a teacher getting tossed off the plane—which explodes moments later.

Hero—Dustin Hoffman is a small-time crook who saves Geena Davis from the wreckage of a crashed plane.

Passenger 57—Air marshal Wesley Snipes does battle with hijackers, including Elizabeth Hurley as a flight attendant with a serious attitude.

Planes, Trains & Automobiles—Not exactly an advertisement for the travel industry.

Rain Man—Dustin Hoffman's autistic character is so petrified of flying that he has a meltdown in an airport.

Twilight Zone: The Movie—In one segment, John Lithgow plays a nervous flier who sees a gremlin ripping up the engine on the wing right outside his window.

5 things that happen in a movie home at the start of the day

5 things that happen in a movie home at the start of the day

1. The newspaper never makes it to the front stoop. It usually gets tossed into the bushes, or on the lawn just as the automatic sprinkler goes on, or even onto the roof.

2. When the main character wakes up, he will try to make love to his conveniently lipsticked and rouged wife, but the kids and the dog will burst in before they can truly get busy. If there are no kids or dog, the phone will ring and it will be the boss, telling our hero, "I don't care if it's your day off, I need you to be downtown in 20 minutes."

3. Everyone in the family will need to use the bathroom at the same time. (Even if it's a two-story, four-bedroom house, there will be just the one main bathroom.)

4. Mom will cook a hearty breakfast for everyone, but no one will have time to eat. The kids will gobble a spoonful of cereal or slug down a glass of orange juice while grabbing their lunches and saying they're late for school, and the hubby will adjust his tie and say he's only got time for coffee as he comes bounding down the stairs.

5. As our hero exits, his wife will come after him and give him a playful squeeze or a lusty kiss, mostly for the benefit of the nosy neighbor across the street, who will shake her head in disgust.

16 movies

that were

far too

long

16 movies that were far too long

Anna and the King (1999) — 148 minutes

Armageddon (1998) — 144 minutes

Around the World in 80 Days (1956) — 175 minutes

The Evening Star (1996) — 129 minutes

For the Boys (1991) — 138 minutes

The Green Mile (1991) — 188 minutes

Hamlet (1996) — 242 minutes

Heaven's Gate (1980) — 219 minutes

The Horse Whisperer (1998) — 170 minutes

Independence Day (1996) — 145 minutes

Meet Joe Black (1998) — 178 minutes

The Messenger: The Story of Joan of Arc (1999) — 160 minutes

Midnight in the Garden of Good and Evil (1997) — 155 minutes

Robin Hood: Prince of Thieves (1991) — 143 minutes

Sleepers (1996) 147 minutes

A Time to Kill (1996) — 149 minutes

15 terrific movies with a running time of less than 100 minutes

15 terrific movies with a running time of less than 100 minutes

Annie Hall (1977) — 93 minutes

The Blair Witch Project (1999) — 86 minutes

Brief Encounter (1946) — 86 minutes

City Lights (1931) — 87 minutes

Dumbo (1941) — 64 minutes

The General (1927) — 75 minutes

High Noon (1952) — 85 minutes

His Girl Friday (1940) — 92 minutes

A Night in Casablanca (1946) — 85 minutes

Nosferatu (1922) — 94 minutes

Persona (1966) — 85 minutes

The Public Enemy (1931) — 83 minutes

Run Lola Run (1999) — 80 minutes

Sullivan's Travels (1934) — 90 minutes

Zelig (1983) — 79 minutes

in-jokes

in-jokes

filmmakers and actors have always loved to insert sly little inside jokes into their movies. Sometimes they're winking at their own images, sometimes they're paying tribute to a mentor, sometimes they're referencing their own earlier work. And sometimes they're just goofin' because they can.

In *His Girl Friday*, Cary Grant invokes his own real name when he tells a politician, "The last person who threatened me was Archie Leach and two weeks later he slit his own throat." Later in the film, Grant says that a character played by Ralph Bellamy "looks just like Ralph Bellamy." In *American Graffiti*, the license plate on one of the cars is THX 1138—the title of a sci-fi movie made by George Lucas when he was a film student. In one form or another, the THX 1138 combo appears in a number of other Lucas productions, including the *Indiana Jones* and *Star Wars* movies.

Some of my favorite in-jokes:

Blade Runner
One of the buildings in the skyline is the Millennium Falcon from Star Wars.

Close Encounters of the Third Kind
When an alien spaceship soars right over Richard Dreyfuss's head, R2-D2 can be seen attached to the ship, hanging upside down.

Coming to America

In a dual cameo appearance, Ralph Bellamy and Don Ameche reprise their roles as the Duke brothers from an earlier Eddie Murphy–John Landis film, Trading Places.

Ferris Bueller's Day Off

All of the license plates are acronyms for previous films by John Hughes: VCTN for National Lampoon's Vacation, MMOM for Mr. Mom, TBC for The Breakfast Club, etc.

Fight Club

There's a movie marquee for a previous Brad Pitt film, Seven Years in Tibet.

Hannibal

In Florence, an investigator who will become a victim of Hannibal's peels and eats an orange—a subtle nod to The Godfather, in which several doomed characters are seen buying or consuming oranges.

Jay and Silent Bob Strike Back

The entire movie is basically one long inside joke, with bountiful cameos by characters from previous Kevin Smith films such as Clerks, Mallrats, and Chasing Amy; multiple slams at Smith's Internet critics; a few digs at Miramax; self-deprecating appearances by directors such as Gus Van Zant; and a hilarious sequence in which Matt Damon and Ben Affleck make fun of each other's movies while they're filming a gratuitously violent sequel to Good Will Hunting.

in-jokes

Magnolia

(WARNING! If you haven't seen the movie, you might want to skip this item.) In a nod to Exodus 8:2, a biblical passage about a plague of frogs, the numbers 8 and 2 appear throughout the film—which ends with thousands of frogs falling from the sky.

Minority Report

Cameos by Vanilla Sky *alums Cameron Diaz and Cameron Crowe.*

Monsters, Inc.

So many sly gags that the double-disc DVD includes an in-joke guide. Just one example: The sushi bar is called "Harryhausen's," a tribute to Ray Harryhausen, creator of stop-motion animation used in such movies as Clash of the Titans *and* Jason and the Argonauts.

Reservoir Dogs

There are several references to other films written or directed by Quentin Tarantino:

Harvey Keitel's character is asked, "How's Alabama?"—the name of Patricia Arquette's character in True Romance.

In Reservoir Dogs, *Mr. Blond's "real" name is Vic Vega. In* Pulp Fiction, *John Travolta's character was Vincent Vega.*

The Vic Vega character in Reservoir Dogs *talks about his parole officer, Scagnetti. That's the name of the corrupt cop who hunts down the suspects in* Natural Born Killers.

And in Reservoir Dogs *there's talk about "unloading the diamonds on a guy named Marcellus." In* Pulp Fiction, *the kingpin played by Ving Rhames is Marcellus Wallace. (Maybe that unseen, glowing bounty in Marcellus's briefcase is the stash of diamonds?)*

Scream

A grown-up Linda Blair from The Exorcist *has a cameo as a reporter.*

Spider-Man

Peter Parker's uncle drives a gold 1973 Oldsmobile Delta 88— director Sam Raimi's own ride, made famous by its appearances in the Evil Dead *movies.*

buried
treasures

buried treasures

 here's something terribly unjust about a world in which more people have seen *Scooby-Doo* than all of these movies put together.

The Big Picture (1989)

Kevin Bacon stars as an aspiring director in this hilarious spoof of Hollywood, directed by Christopher Guest and also featuring Michael McKean, Jennifer Jason Leigh, and Teri Hatcher. Martin Short is a standout as a flamboyant agent who wouldn't know sincerity if it jumped on his lap.

The Claim (2000)

A beautiful and haunting fable starring Peter Mullan as a starving gold miner who sells his wife and infant to another miner and in 20 years' time becomes the richest man in the region, with a stash of gold bars and a beautiful new wife (Milla Jovovich). But his past comes back to haunt him when his former bride (Nastassja Kinski) and his daughter (Sarah Polley) return to town. Snowbound 19th-century scenes evoke memories of the great McCabe & Mrs. Miller.

Dinner Rush (2000)

One of the best movies ever made about the restaurant business. Danny Aiello shines as the patriarch of a popular Italian eatery in New York that has become the darling of the trend set.

With Sandra Bernhard as a pretentious food critic, John Corbett as a mysterious loner at the bar, and Summer Phoenix as a waitress and struggling artist who has to put up with the most pretentious customer in restaurant history.

Go (1999)

Sarah Polley, Katie Holmes, Scott Wolf, and Timothy Olyphant are among the delights in this time-folding tale from director Doug Liman, who has also done Swingers and The Bourne Identity. A crackling, energetic film that's almost as good as its obvious inspiration, Pulp Fiction.

Happy Accidents (2000)

Marisa Tomei falls in love with Vincent D'Onofrio, who claims to be a visitor from the distant future—but she's been so unlucky in love that not even this news is enough to drive her away. Still, she has to come to terms with the fact that D'Onofrio is obviously insane, because the only other possible explanation is that he really IS from the future—and that can't be the case, right? Happy Accidents keeps you guessing to the very end.

Judgment Night (1993)

Denis Leary is wonderfully menacing as a killer who stalks yuppies Emilio Estevez and Cuba Gooding, Jr., through the West Side of Chicago.

Punchline (1988)

Despite the star power of Tom Hanks and Sally Field, this biting and very inside look at the darker side of the world of stand-up comedy was a box office disappointment—but it's well worth a rental. Hanks plays a brilliant but troubled rising star on the stand-

buried treasures

up circuit who strikes up an unusual friendship with a housewife (Fields), a Roseanne-type figure who escapes the family kitchen for the terrifying but exhilarating world of open mike night.

The Salton Sea (2000)

Val Kilmer as a jazz trumpeter whose life is shattered when his wife is caught in the cross fire of a drug-fueled gun battle. Within a year, Kilmer has degenerated into a crystal meth addict who scratches out a living as a police informant—but it's all part of an elaborate, twisted plan to seek redemption.

When We Were Kings (1996)

Will Smith's Oscar-nominated performance as Ali shrinks in comparison to the real deal—Muhammad Ali preparing to do battle with the heavily favored George Foreman in Zaire in 1974. This documentary captures Ali in all his glorious, blustery charisma as he runs through the streets surrounded by thousands of adoring fans and puts a serious psych job on the glowering Foreman before pulling off one of the most shocking upsets in boxing history.

movies
about
estranged
couples
who
reunite in
a time of
crisis

movies about estranged couples who reunite in a time of crisis

Sometimes it takes more than a marriage counselor and a couple of apologies to get an estranged couple back together. At the outset of each of these thrillers, a romance is in tatters and there's no chance for reconciliation—that is, until the bickering twosome is thrust together in a time of great stress and must team up to save lives and escape certain death. Only then do they admit what everyone else has known all along: that they're made for each other.

The Abyss (1989)

Ed Harris is the head of an oil-drilling crew and Mary Elizabeth Mastrantonio is an engineer, and they drive each other crazy—until they're faced with a possible nuclear explosion and some translucent and evil water creatures. At that point they restate their mutual love.

Die Hard (1988)

Bruce Willis is New York cop John McClane, who heads to L.A. in an effort to patch things up with his wife, played by Bonnie Bedelia, who has reclaimed her maiden name and is fending off the advances of a slimy co-worker. After they team up to thwart a team of terrorists led by that wacky Hans Gruber, they melt into each other's arms.

Jurassic Park III (2001)

Téa Leoni has left husband William Macy and has a new "friend"—a guy who takes Leoni's and Macy's son parasailing and winds up as a dangling skeleton. Macy and Leoni arrive on the island to search for their son, and as they do battle with all sorts of prehistoric-lookin' beasts like a 44-foot spinosaurus, they realize that if they ever get off that crazy island, they'll spend the rest of their lives together.

The Last Boy Scout (1991)

Bruce Willis again, this time as a former Secret Service agent whose wife, played by Chelsea Field, is cheating on him with his best friend. After the bad guys are blown up, Willis spews a stream of obscenities in Field's ear—his way of saying he still loves her. They embrace.

Nighthawks (1981)

Sylvester Stallone is a workaholic cop estranged from wife Lindsay Wagner. Only after her life is endangered by bad guy Rutger Hauer do Stallone and Wagner get back together.

Ocean's 11 (2001)

George Clooney's fresh out of prison and planning two major heists: 1. He aims to relieve three Las Vegas casinos of about $100 million. 2. He intends to win back the heart of former girlfriend Julia Roberts, who's now hooked up with evil kingpin Andy Garcia. After much bickering and bantering, Roberts tells Clooney to stay out of her life and Clooney promises he'll leave her alone—and that's the moment when we know they'll end up together.

Outbreak (1995)

Dustin Hoffman and Rene Russo break up and get on with their lives—but they're reunited when they do battle with a deadly virus that threatens to wipe out half the population.

movies about estranged couples who reunite in a time of crisis

Running Scared (1986)

Billy Crystal is the cop, Darlanne Fluegel is the estranged wife. You know the rest of the drill.

Twister (1996)

Tornado chaser Bill Paxton dumps uptight fiancée Jami Gertz and gets back together with fellow adventure-seeker Helen Hunt.

Unbreakable (2000)

Bruce Willis is at it again, this time as a security guard with a mysterious gift who is separated from wife Robin Wright Penn. By the end of the movie, after much trauma and danger, they have, of course, reunited.

actors
and
their
pet
causes

actors and their pet causes

Woody Allen

    Against colorization of classic films.

Alec Baldwin

    Freeing horses from a lifetime of pulling carriages through Manhattan.

Marlon Brando

    When Brando won the Academy Award in 1973 for The Godfather, *he sent one "Sacheen Littlefeather," birth name Maria Cruz, to the podium to announce Brando was refusing the Oscar to protest the negative portrayals of Native Americans in movies. Littlefeather capitalized on her brief moment in the spotlight by posing nude for* Playboy.

Ted Danson

    Environmental issues.

Michael Douglas

    In favor of nuclear disarmament.

Michael J. Fox

    Parkinson's disease.

Richard Gere

    Freedom for the people of Tibet.

Melanie Griffith

Protection of large, exotic animals. (Including Antonio Banderas, one presumes.)

Goldie Hawn

Circus elephants. In March 2000, Hawn wrote a letter to legislators in her native state of Maryland, stating, "Circus elephants are denied almost everything important to them, including family relationships, privacy, mental stimulation, physical exercise and emotional outlets." You gotta love a woman who's concerned about the privacy rights of elephants.

Madonna

Voter registration. She wrapped herself in the American flag and told MTV viewers, "If you don't vote, you're going to get a spanky!" (Subsequent research has failed to locate where Madonna may have cast her ballots.)

Paul Newman

All proceeds from his Newman's Own products go to charity. In 20 years, more than $125 million has been donated to various causes.

Rosie O'Donnell

Supports the social and intellectual development of underserved kids.

Christopher Reeve

Research to develop treatment and find a cure for paralysis.

Julia Roberts

Funding for more research on Rett Syndrome.

actors and their pet causes

Steven Spielberg
Starbright Foundation.

Meryl Streep
Against chemicals in apples.

I could go the rest of my life without seeing any more variations on the following scenes

I could go the rest of my life without seeing any more variations on the following scenes

After hailing a cab, getting caught in traffic, jumping out of the cab, running through the streets, hijacking a moped and racing through the airport, the guy catches up with the gal just as she's about to board the plane, and he tells her that he loves her and he doesn't want her to go away because she completes him or whatever. The smiling flight attendants close the door to the ramp and the plane takes off, as the young lovers make out in the terminal.

A seemingly defenseless little old lady defends herself by kicking the bad guy in the balls.

A seemingly defenseless *young* lady defends herself by kicking the bad guy in the balls.

A seemingly defenseless little kid defends himself by kicking the bad guy in the shins.

In a crowded public square, a couple gets into a nasty, loud fight, but then reconciles—and everyone around them breaks into applause.

During a practice run on the track, a group of cocky, macho race car drivers (or motorcyclists) are blown away by a mystery driver with reckless tendencies. Just when one of the macho guys is about to punch the new young punk, the mystery driver takes off "his" helmet—and a mane of beautiful hair falls free. It's a girl!

Any and all musical montages showing the weakling getting whipped into shape.

A year after his wife has disappeared, a man sees a woman in a crowd who looks and dresses like his wife. He chases her through the streets, finally catches up to her, says, "Honey!" and taps her on the shoulder—and she turns around and looks at him as if he's nuts. "Sorry," he says. "I thought you were someone else."

A rogue hero gets shot in the shoulder and it doesn't even slow him down—but later, when his girlfriend pours alcohol on the wound and sews him up, he winces and howls in pain, and she teases him about being a big baby.

Dogs who greet visitors by sniffing their crotches.

At the conclusion of a brutal rooftop duel, the good guy is hanging over the ledge and the bad guy is cackling about this turn of events. And that's when the good guy makes a quick move and throws the bad guy over the ledge while somehow managing to maintain his balance just long enough for the girl to regain consciousness, race over, and pull him to safety.

Somebody points a gun, and everyone says, "Whoa, take it easy!" Then, to prove how serious he/she is, the gun-wielding character cocks the trigger. When this happens, we know the gun will not be fired and reason will prevail.

An attractive woman is alone in a bar when a handsome cad approaches and tries to hit on her, much to the amusement of several guys who have already been shut down. She explains to this new guy

I could go the rest of my life without seeing any more variations on the following scenes

that she's happily married, but he keeps hitting on her. Just when we figure she's going to throw her drink in his face, she wraps her arms around him and gives him a sexy smooch. Surprise, surprise, they're husband and wife!

19 movies featuring Larry King making a cameo as ... Larry King!

19 movies featuring Larry King making a cameo as . . . Larry King!

a merica's most celebrity-friendly interviewer gets more movie work than Gene Hackman. Usually we get just a glimpse of King on his familiar set, pitching a softball or two in the direction of a fictional character—but in *America's Sweethearts* he had an expanded role that included a rugged interrogation of the self-centered actress played by Catherine Zeta-Jones. Given that King is never that tough on guests in real life, it was a hell of an acting job.

King's cameos:

An Alan Smithee Film: Burn Hollywood Burn (1997)

America's Sweethearts (2001)

Bulworth (1998)

Contact (1997)

The Contender (2000)

Courage Under Fire (1996)

Crazy People (1990)

Dave (1993)

Disney's The Kid (2000)

Eddie and the Cruisers II: Eddie Lives! (1989)

Enemy of the State (1998)

The Exorcist III (1990)

Ghostbusters (1984)

The Jackal (1997)

John Q (2002)

The Long Kiss Goodnight (1996)

Mad City (1997)

Open Season (1996)

Primary Colors (1998)

For years King would tout films in his *USA Today* column, which wasn't really a column—it was more like a collection of the random thoughts that popped into the man's head between the time he zipped up at the urinal and headed over to the sink to wash his hands. ("Chocolate or vanilla? I can't decide . . . If there's a better-looking woman than Julie Christie, I'd sure like to meet her . . . Look up 'class' in the dictionary, you'll find a picture of Sandy Koufax . . .") Often, King would use the column to shill for a movie in which he just happened to have a cameo—but, true to his journalistic instincts, King would always inform the readers of this fact before assuring us that it had no bearing whatsoever on his opinion that the film in question was "the funniest movie to come down the pike in a long time." As chronicled by The Hotline's "Last Call" column, here's what King had to say about three films that came down his pike:

July 16, 2001:

"I have a cameo role in the movie America's Sweethearts, *opening Friday. That said, it is one of the funniest comedies to come down the pike in years."*

April 26, 1993:

"Put aside the fact that I make a cameo appearance in the film Dave. *Ivan Reitman's latest is one of the funniest movies to come down the pike in a long, long time."*

19 movies featuring Larry King making a cameo as . . . Larry King!

March 19, 1990:

"Even though I appear as myself in the upcoming film Crazy People, *you'll have to take my objective view that it's one of the funniest movies to come down the pike in a long, long time."*

Larry King:

One of the funniest blurbmeisters to come down the pike in a long, long time.

7 movies in which Ben Affleck cries like a big fat baby

7 movies in which Ben Affleck cries like a big fat baby

ben Affleck started his career playing wise-asses and weasels, but now that he's got the capped teeth and the chiseled physique and the shirtless magazine covers and the string of hot celebrity girlfriends, there's no doubt that he's pure leading man. Only one thing: Nearly every movie Affleck does turns into *The Crying Game*. He wept in *Chasing Amy*, he blubbered in *Armageddon*, he let the tears flow in *Reindeer Games*, he broke down in *Bounce*, he lost it in *Pearl Harbor*, and he teared up twice in 2002, in *The Sum of All Fears* and *Changing Lanes*. (And in four of those movies, he was wailing over the loss of male friends, for crying out loud.) I know it's the 21st century and it's OK for a man to show his emotions, but I don't think Judy Garland wept onscreen this much in her entire career. And I *know* Steve McQueen didn't.

Armageddon (1998)

When Bruce Willis sacrifices himself to save the planet and to spare Affleck, Ben breaks down.

Ben: "Harry! Harry! You can't do this to me! It's my job!"

Bruce: "You're gonna take care of my little girl now. That's your job. Always thought of you as a son. Always. And I'd be damn proud to have you marry Grace. Take care of yourself."

Ben (between sobs): "No Harry! I love you!"

Bruce: "Good-bye, son."

Bounce (2000)

Ben falls in love with Gwyneth Paltrow—and tears up three times in the process.

Changing Lanes (2002)

Amanda Peet tells Ben she knew all about his affair with Toni Collette—but she loves him anyway and will stand by him. A single tear streams down Ben's face.

Chasing Amy (1997)

After a huge fight with Joey Lauren Adams, Ben goes back to his apartment and puts on some sad music. A single tear streams down Ben's face. Again.

Pearl Harbor (2001)

Ben can't fight the tears as he holds dying best friend Josh Hartnett in his arms.

Reindeer Games (2000)

Ben can't fight the tears as he holds dying best friend James Frain in his arms.

The Sum of All Fears (2002)

Ben gets misty and ALMOST breaks down when Morgan Freeman bites it.

age
difference
between
Michael
Douglas
and his
leading
ladies

age difference between Michael Douglas and his leading ladies

ichael Douglas is one of my favorite actors because he dives headfirst into all of his projects, whether it's quality fare such as *The China Syndrome, Wonder Boys,* and *Traffic,* or big-budget trash like *Don't Say a Word, A Perfect Murder,* and *Basic Instinct.* Even when Douglas knows he's starring in high-gloss junk, he'll never wink at the camera à la Burt Reynolds to let us in on the joke. He plays it straight and he plays it hard, thus elevating even something as ludicrously overwrought as *The Game,* in which he plays a kazillionaire whose younger brother (Sean Penn) sets him up for the most elaborate practical joke of all time—a joke involving at least 500 people in California and Mexico.

Douglas often plays the sweater-clad, elbow-patched, smugly successful urbanite whose world is turned upside down when he makes one horrific decision, whether it's entering into an affair with Glenn Close in *Fatal Attraction,* trusting Charlie Sheen in *Wall Street,* or outfitting the front door of his million-dollar apartment with a cheap lock in *Don't Say a Word.*

But a weird thing is happening. Michael Douglas has chosen to remain stuck at about 45 or so in movie after movie—almost always with a 30ish wife and/or a nubile girlfriend who worships everything about him, and a child or two, usually younger than 10. That's the guy Douglas played in *Fatal Attraction* in 1987, and it's the same guy he played in *Don't Say a Word* in 2001. The only difference is that Anne Archer and Glenn Close are long gone from lead actress consideration because they have committed the unpardonable sin of aging—so these days it's Famke Janssen slipping under the sheets with Douglas, and a new child actor playing the part of the adorable child.

Pretty soon the actress who played Douglas's daughter in *Fatal Attraction* will be old enough to play his wife in a film.

In early films such as *Romancing the Stone* and *It's My Turn*, Douglas was roughly the same age as co-stars Kathleen Turner and Jill Clayburgh. Today, those great actresses have to play the mothers of twentysomethings—but Michael Douglas still gets the plum leading roles, opposite women who are at least 20 years his junior. (In real life, Douglas exited his marriage with age-peer wife Diandra and married Catherine Zeta-Jones, who is 25 years younger than him. Jones's father is just two years younger than Douglas.)

Here are some of Douglas's most famous roles, with his age and the ages of his leading gals.

Basic Instinct

Douglas: 48
Sharon Stone: 34
Jeanne Tripplehorn: 29

Disclosure

Douglas: 50
Demi Moore: 32

The American President

Douglas: 51
Annette Bening: 37

age difference between Michael Douglas and his leading ladies

The Game
Douglas: 53

Deborah Kara Unger: 31

A Perfect Murder
Douglas: 54

Gwyneth Paltrow: 26

Wonder Boys
Douglas: 56

Frances McDormand: 43

Katie Holmes: 21

Don't Say a Word
Douglas: 57

Famke Janssen: 37

12 legendary actors who were in movies with O.J. Simpson before he "didn't" kill his wife and her friend and was basically kicked out of show business

12 legendary actors who were in movies with O.J. Simpson before he "didn't" kill his wife and her friend and was basically kicked out of show business

Fred Astaire

Richard Burton

Faye Dunaway

Ava Gardner

Lillian Gish

Richard Harris

William Holden

Burt Lancaster

Sophia Loren

Lee Marvin

Steve McQueen

Paul Newman

Note: Loren, Gardner, Lancaster, and Harris were in The Cassandra Crossing. *Gish was in* Hambone and Hillie. *McQueen, Newman, Holden, Dunaway, and Astaire were in* The Towering Inferno. *Marvin and Burton were in* The Klansman.

movies
set in
Chicago
but
filmed in
Toronto

movies set in Chicago but filmed in Toronto

n the opening sequence of the 2001 mystery-romance *Angel Eyes*, we see the aftermath of a terrible car wreck, as Toronto's famous CN Tower looms in the background. This would not be a problem—except the movie is set in Chicago, not Toronto. Later we see a Toronto Transit bus zipping down the streets of the Windy City. And in a scene where Jennifer Lopez and Jim Caviezel take a leisurely evening stroll, they walk past the neon-lit Toronto department store known as "Honest Ed's."

Sloppy sloppy sloppy. But that's what happens when filmmakers cut expenses by trying to pass off Toronto as Chicago, a trend that shows no signs of abating. Each of the following movies contains scenes set in Chicago—but filmed mostly in Toronto.

My Big Fat Greek Wedding (2002)

John Q (2002)

Lakeboat (2000)

Angel Eyes (2001)

Driven (2001)

On the Line (2001)

The Ladies Man (2000)

Three to Tango (1999)

Blues Brothers 2000 (1998)

Guilty as Sin (1993)

Adventures in Babysitting (1987)

The Big Town (1987)

Till Death Do Us Part (yet to be released)

There's also the adaptation of a long-running stage hit, a musical starring Catherine Zeta-Jones and Renée Zellweger.

It's called *Chicago*. Some scenes were shot in Chicago. The bulk of the film was shot in . . . Toronto.

13 great perks of being a movie character

13 great perks of being a movie character

1. You can always find a legal parking spot right in front of your destination, even if you're driving in Manhattan on a weekday.

2. If you need to disguise yourself as a hospital worker, security guard, or janitor, just knock out the first such employee you encounter. (A simple blow to the back of the head does it every time.) Their clothes will fit you perfectly.

3. Speaking of clothes, the outfit you wore the night before will look great if you just drape it over the chair, next to the bed.

4. When you walk into a restaurant, there's always a great table available near the window. And once you've ordered, your food will arrive within two minutes.

5. You never have to do laundry—unless you're in a romantic comedy, in which case you'll have to do your laundry in a safe and squeaky-clean place populated by quirky and lovable eccentrics, including at least one really good-looking and conveniently available person.

6. Even if you're stinking drunk, a few cups of coffee will sober you right up.

7. No matter how fast you pound a keyboard, you'll never make a tyop—I mean, a typo.

8. Whatever you buy at the store, you'll always have the exact amount handy, and it will never involve any loose change.

9. Your credit card can be used to unlock any door in the world.

10. You don't have to say good-bye when you're on the phone. The person on the other end of the line will instinctively know when the conversation is over, and will gently hang up and then sit motionless while staring into space, contemplating what you've just said.

11. If you're shot in the shoulder or the knee, just clean and wrap the wound and you're good to go. You'll never go into shock or pass out from a loss of blood, and the wound will never become infected.

12. When you go to a ballgame, you'll always have great seats, and an exciting play will occur only after you and your friend have had a chance to discuss something. Plus, your chances of catching a foul ball are roughly 50–50.

13. If you put on a bulletproof vest, you will not get shot in the legs or the face.

9 rules
of
drinking
in the
movies

9 rules of drinking in the movies

1. If you walk into a bar and order a generic "beer," the bartender will always take your order without asking the obvious question: "What KIND of beer do you want?"

2. However, if a brewery has paid a product placement fee, you and every other character in the movie will drink only that brand of beer, and you'll always make sure the label is facing the camera. Billboards and signs advertising the beer will conveniently appear in the background, no matter where you go. It'll be as if that beer is the only beer in the world.

3. In Westerns, everyone drinks whiskey in the middle of the day, even if it's 100 degrees, and saloons are always filled with poker players and dance-hall girls.

4. Even if you've never been in a bar before, if you order a shot and tell the bartender, "Leave the bottle right there!" he'll do so without a word—but he'll hover nearby, cleaning a small section of the bar top with a towel, in case you want to talk about your problems.

5. Characters who get drunk for the first time will always do something really wild, like leading the entire bar crowd in a sing-along or doing a striptease at the company party, or confessing

their love for someone they've always hated. When they wake up in the morning, they'll be hungover and they won't remember a thing. By midday, however, they're feeling great again.

6. Bartenders are always great sources of information—but only after you slip them a $20 bill.

7. If you get into a barroom brawl, the police won't show up until the place has been completely wrecked—and even when 100 cops arrive on the scene, you'll be able to sneak out the back way (with the help of a perky waitress who has a crush on you).

8. At high school parties, the biggest guy on the football team is always the one who guzzles the most booze and passes out first, usually facefirst into a giant bowl of dip.

9. In the history of movies, when a bartender says, "Don't you think you've had enough!" nobody has ever said, "Good point! I've got to get up early tomorrow. Thanks for the advice!"

6 differences between the movie version of the world of TV and real TV

6 differences between the movie version of the world of TV and real TV

1. In the movie version, whenever a character makes a big confession or gives an unrehearsed speech on live television, the director always says, "Stay with her!" to the camera crew, and he leans forward, anticipating some landmark television.

In reality, if somebody started to have a nervous breakdown on live TV, the director would go to a commercial.

2. In the movie version of TV, as the speech is being delivered, we see all the other major and supporting characters watching TV, whether they're home, at the airport, in a bar, or at a health club.

In reality, not everyone is watching TV all the time—and even if they are in front of the tube, they might be tuned to another channel.

3. In the movie version, once the speech is over, everyone bursts into applause and a moment later the director says, "The network just called and the phones are ringing off the hook!"

In reality, once the speech is over, there would be awkward silence, and then the floor director would say, "I don't know how to tell you this, but we cut to a commercial five minutes ago."

4. In the movie version, every TV news reporter is an unethical glory hound willing to lie to friends, bribe sources, jeopardize investigations, endanger lives, and break laws in order to get a scoop.

In reality, most field reporters are hardworking and scrupulous. I'm serious!

5. In the movie version, newsrooms are always overflowing with ultra-busy, well-dressed people who are walking around with a great sense of purpose while holding stacks of files. The phones are constantly ringing, and there's always a secretary standing by to give the star reporter a fresh cup of coffee and a stack of messages the moment he or she walks in.

In reality, newsrooms are often sparsely populated, as reporters and producers are out gathering stories. If the phone rings, someone answers it, or it goes into voicemail.

And if you want coffee or your messages, get them yourself.

6. In the movie version, the anchor team always consists of a distinguished, white-haired gentleman who's something of a pompous jerk and a big-haired younger woman who's always perky.

In reality, the anchor team consists of—

Okay, maybe they got that one right.

the
ugliest
drag
queens in
movie
history

the ugliest drag queens in movie history

 n alphabetical order. To rank them would be to admit I find some less hideous than others, and I'm not prepared to do that.

Michael Caine in *Dressed to Kill* (1980)

Charlie Chaplin in *A Woman* (1915)

Divine in *Pink Flamingos* (1972)

Cary Grant in *I Was a Male War Bride* (1949)

Gene Hackman in *The Birdcage* (1996)

Dustin Hoffman in *Tootsie* (1982)

Philip Seymour Hoffman in *Flawless* (1999)

Martin Lawrence in *Big Momma's House* (2000)

Jack Lemmon in *Some Like It Hot* (1959)

Jerry Lewis in *Three on a Couch* (1966)

John Lithgow in *The World According to Garp* (1982)

Eddie Murphy as Mrs. Klump in *The Nutty Professor* (1996)

Miguel Nuñez, Jr. in *Juwanna Mann* (2002)

Wesley Snipes, John Leguizamo, and Patrick Swayze in
   To Wong Foo, Thanks for Everything, Julie Newmar (1995)

Robin Williams in *Mrs. Doubtfire* (1993)

Ed Wood in *Glen or Glenda?* (1953)

the 12
best
movies
about the
newspaper
business

the 12 best movies about the newspaper business

Absence of Malice (1981)

All the President's Men (1976)

Citizen Kane (1941)

Continental Divide (1981)

Deadline—U.S.A. (1952)

The Front Page (1931)

His Girl Friday (1940)

The Mean Season (1985)

Meet John Doe (1941)

The Paper (1994)

The Parallax View (1974)

Teacher's Pet (1958)

Note: The three worst newspaper movies of recent years are Never Been Kissed, I Love Trouble, *and* Straight Talk. *They're accurate about journalism in the same way that* Peter Pan *is accurate about air travel.*

the 10 best Easter movies

the 10 best Easter movies

rom *Miracle on 34th Street* to *A Christmas Carol* to *It's a Wonderful Life* to *How the Grinch Stole Christmas*, there are dozens upon dozens of beloved and popular Christmas-themed movies—but with the exception of such turgid claptrap as *The Robe* and not-really-about-Jesus movies such as *Ben-Hur*, precious few Easter-themed films have become perennial springtime favorites—or for that matter, deserve such status. But there are a few notable exceptions. The best movies ever made about the adult Jesus and/or the Christian holiday celebrating his resurrection:

1. *Jesus Christ Superstar* (1973)
2. *The Last Temptation of Christ* (1988)
3. *The Life of Brian* (1979)
4. *The Greatest Story Ever Told* (1965)
5. *The King of Kings* (1927 version directed by Cecil B. DeMille)
6. *Dogma* (1999)
7. *Easter Parade* (1948)
8. *Jesus of Montreal* (1989)
9. *King of Kings* (1961)
10. *Godspell* (1973)

Honorable mention: Jesus of Nazareth *(TV mini-series directed by Franco Zeffirelli)*

this is why they need screen-writers

this is why they need screenwriters

ime after time at the Academy Awards, some of the most accomplished thespians in the world prove just how much they need screenwriters—or at least a friend to tap them on the shoulder and say, "You're not making any sense, darling."

In reverse chronological order, some of the most embarrassing and appalling speeches in Oscar telecast history:

2002—

Before presenting the Best Actor award, Julia Roberts gushes about having just met Sidney Poitier and then takes a gratuitous shot at "Tom Conti," the orchestra conductor who tried to get her to cut short her own acceptance speech the year before. (She means Bill Conti. Tom Conti is an actor.) Then Roberts opens the envelope and tells the world, "I love my life," before announcing Denzel Washington's name. After Washington's speech, Roberts clings to him like a lusty cheerleader as he tries to walk off the stage and find his wife.

1998—

After ordering the audience to observe a moment of silence for the real-life victims of the Titanic, *director James Cameron hoists his Oscar to the sky and says, "I'm the king of the world!"*

1993—

Presenter Richard Gere pleads with the entire world to join him in communicating telepathically with Chinese leader Deng Xiao-ping: "Something miraculous and really kind of movielike here could happen. We could all send our love and truth . . . that he will take his troops . . . away from Tibet and allow these people to live as free, independent people again." Not since Tinkerbell was brought back to life has there been such an onstage plea.

1992—

Everyone remembers Jack Palance dropping down to do those one-armed push-ups, but before that stunt, Palance filled our heads with regrettable imagery, by saying of City Slickers co-star and Oscar host Billy Crystal, "I crap bigger than him." Great.

1985—

It almost seems like piling on to mention it any more, but it's Sally Field's fault for saying it in the first place: "The first time [I won] I didn't feel it, but this time I feel it, and I can't deny the fact that you like me, right now, you like me!"

1979—

In a speech that sounds great but makes absolutely no sense, Laurence Olivier says his honorary Oscar "must be seen as a beautiful star in that firmament which shines upon me at this moment, dazzling me a little, but filling me with warmth of the extraordinary elation, the euphoria that happens to so many of us at the first breath of the majestic glow of a new tomorrow."

And in the audience, Gary Busey was thinking, "Hey, that's what I was going to say!"

this is why they need screenwriters

1978—

Shirley MacLaine addresses brother Warren Beatty: *"Imagine what you could accomplish if you tried celibacy!"* Beatty grimaces while girlfriend Diane Keaton slumps in her chair.

1978—

Vanessa Redgrave accepts the Best Supporting Actress award for Julia and thanks the Academy for voting for her *"despite the efforts of a small band of Zionist hoodlums."*

1973—

When Marlon Brando's name is announced as Best Actor for The Godfather, a B-movie actress named Maria Cruz, calling herself *"Sacheen Littlefeather,"* takes the podium and says, *"I think the awards in this country at this time are inappropriate to receive or give until the condition of the American Indian is drastically altered."* What this has to do with Marlon Brando winning a trophy for playing a gangster has never been explained.

best films that didn't win the Academy Award for best picture

best films that didn't win the Academy Award for best picture

1941

Winner: *How Green Was My Valley*

Should have won: *Citizen Kane* or *The Maltese Falcon*

1952

Winner: *The Greatest Show on Earth*

Should have won: *High Noon* or *The Quiet Man*

1956

Winner: *Around the World in 80 Days*

Should have won: *Giant* or *Friendly Persuasion*

1961

Winner: *West Side Story*

Should have won: *The Hustler*

1967

Winner: *In the Heat of the Night*

Should have won: *Bonnie and Clyde*

1979

Winner: *Kramer vs. Kramer*

Should have won: *Apocalypse Now*

1980

Winner: *Ordinary People*

Should have won: *Raging Bull*

1982

Winner: *Gandhi*

Should have won: *E.T.* or *The Verdict* or *Tootsie*

1989

Winner: *Driving Miss Daisy*

Should have won: *Born on the Fourth of July* or *Field of Dreams*

1990

Winner: *Dances with Wolves*

Should have won: *GoodFellas*

1994

Winner: *Forrest Gump*

Should have won: *Pulp Fiction* or *The Shawshank Redemption*

1998

Winner: *Shakespeare in Love*

Should have won: *Saving Private Ryan*

2000

Winner: *Gladiator*

Should have won: *Crouching Tiger, Hidden Dragon* or *Traffic*

not even
nominated

not even nominated

a t least the films in the previous list were nominated for Best Picture—but these classics, some of which often appear on lists of the greatest movies ever made, weren't even considered among the top five pictures of their respective years.

City Lights (1931)

Duck Soup (1933)

The Thirty-Nine Steps (1935)

Rules of the Game (1939)

His Girl Friday (1940)

Sullivan's Travels (1942)

To Have and Have Not (1944)

My Darling Clementine (1946)

Singin' in the Rain (1952)

Rear Window (1954)

Some Like It Hot (1959)

Psycho (1960)

2001: A Space Odyssey (1968)

McCabe & Mrs. Miller (1971)

Saturday Night Fever (1977)

Manhattan (1979)

Do the Right Thing (1989)

Reservoir Dogs (1992)

Hoop Dreams (1994)

Memento (2000)

4 actors who were nominated for Academy Awards in the "**wrong**" category

4 actors who were nominated for Academy Awards in the "wrong" category

he Academy of Motion Picture Arts and Sciences has all sorts of complicated rules that must be followed when members are voting for the Oscars—but oddly enough, there's no strict set of guidelines for determining which roles are leads and which roles are supporting. No arbitrary cutoff that says if someone is onscreen for, say, 50 percent or more of a particular movie, then the role has to be considered a lead. It's always been up to the voters to determine the category—but after Barry Fitzgerald was nominated in both categories in 1944 for *Going My Way*, the Academy said that if an actor ever again finished in the top five as a lead and a supporting performer for the same role, the actor would get the nomination in the category in which he or she garnered the most votes.

In the meantime, there have been at least three occasions where the nominees were in the "wrong" categories:

Jennifer Connelly in *A Beautiful Mind* (2001)

This was clearly a lead performance, but studio ads touted Connelly as a candidate for Supporting Actress. She was nominated—and she won against a field of fine actresses who had much smaller roles in their respective films.

Anthony Hopkins in *Silence of the Lambs* (1991)

It's one of the most memorable performances in modern screen history—but Hopkins was onscreen for a total of about 20 minutes. Scott Glenn's FBI agent had more scenes. Nevertheless, Hopkins was a nominee and a winner for Best Actor.

Marlon Brando and Al Pacino in _The Godfather_ (1972)

Brando was nominated, and won, for Best Actor, while Pacino was nominated in the supporting category, even though Pacino had considerably more screen time than Brando.

On second thought, the Academy would like that trophy back...

on second thought, the Academy would like that trophy back ...

 wful movies starring Academy Award–winning actors, AFTER they'd won the Oscar:

BASEketball (1998)

Ernest Borgnine (Academy Award winner for Marty) plays Ted Denslow, owner of the Milwaukee Beers of the National BASEketball League, who chokes on a hot dog and dies. In a videotaped reading of his will, Borgnine sings "I'm Too Sexy" while rubbing ointment on his chest.

The Crew (2000)

Richard Dreyfuss (Oscar winner for The Goodbye Girl) as a member of an aging gang of crooks in Florida who get back into the life and discover that they're not funny or interesting.

Dracula's Dog (1978)

José Ferrer (who won the Academy Award for Cyrano de Bergerac) in the story of a bloodthirsty mutt.

Jury Duty (1995)

Shelley Winters (AA winner for A Patch of Blue) in a Pauly Shore movie. Say no more.

Mama Dracula (1980)

Louise Fletcher (Oscar for *One Flew Over the Cuckoo's Nest*) in the title role in the story of a female vampire who must bathe in the blood of virgins.

Monkeybone (2001)

Whoopi Goldberg (Best Supporting Actress winner for *Ghost*) as Death, whose head explodes. Watching the movie, you know how she feels.

Old Dracula (1974)

David Niven (winner of the Academy Award for *Separate Tables*) as, well, Old Dracula.

Snow Dogs (2002)

Cuba Gooding, Jr. (Best Supporting Actor winner for *Jerry Maguire*) and James Coburn (AA for *Affliction*) appeared in this mushy and dopey kid flick.

The Thing With Two Heads (1972)

Ray Milland (Oscar winner for *The Lost Weekend*) as a bigot whose head is grafted onto the body of Rosie Grier. This follow-up to *The Incredible Two-Headed Transplant* just wasn't as believable as the original.

Thirteen Ghosts (2001)

F. Murray Abraham (*Amadeus*) as a crazy millionaire trying to harness the power of 13 ghosts in order to revive himself from the dead. (Don't ask.)

on second thought, the Academy would like that trophy back . . .

Trog (1970)

Joan Crawford (who won the Academy Award for _Mildred Pierce_) as an old lady scientist who befriends a murderous troglodyte.

The Waterboy (1998)

Kathy Bates (Best Actress winner for _Misery_) as Adam Sandler's trailer trash mom in this idiotic comedy.

red-carpet flubs **and** blunders

by Joan Rivers

red-carpet flubs and blunders
by Joan Rivers

each year at the Academy Awards, Joan Rivers's performance on the red carpet is either charmingly humorous or excruciatingly embarrassing, depending on whether you're amused or horrified when someone is completely out of touch with the event she's covering. Herewith some of Rivers's most entertaining blunders and flubs.

2002—

Rivers repeatedly refers to *Ali,* starring two nominees and named for one of the most famous human beings in modern history, as "Ally," as in "Ally McBeal."

Rivers asks Sidney Poitier, "What was your first movie? *Lilies of the Field?*" Poitier, who had been working in films for 14 years before *Lilies,* replies, "No, my first film was *No Way Out.*"

While interviewing Glenn Close, Rivers mentions that Close is a presenter, when in fact Close and Donald Sutherland are the announcers for the evening. When Close corrects her, Rivers says, "Well, that's because you're up for a nomination for voice," which makes no sense because there is no such category.

Rivers says Jim Broadbent is Australian. He's English.

Rivers gushes about Jennifer Lopez's teeth and then asks the dumbfounded J. Lo, "Are they yours?"

Best Actor nominee (and eventual winner) Denzel Washington is asked by Rivers what it was like to direct himself in *Training Day*. Washington informs her that he did not direct *Training Day*.

Rivers to *Lord of the Rings* star Elijah Wood: "Did you like your nominee basket [of goodies]?" Wood's response: "I'm not nominated."

Is it any wonder that by the time Hugh Grant faced off with Rivers, he smiled and said, "Joan, are you drunk?"

2001—

Nominee Laura Linney is called "Laura Linley."

Rivers tells producers Lucy Fisher and Douglas Wick, "It's so exciting that the two of you produced *Gladiator*." They did not produce *Gladiator*.

Rivers to Catherine Zeta-Jones: "Are you excited about your first nomination?" Zeta-Jones is not nominated.

When the CEO of the E! channel arrives, Rivers bends down and literally kisses the woman's rear end.

Rivers: "People are farting. Brian Dennehey just cut one [and] three cameramen collapsed."

When *Crouching Tiger, Hidden Dragon* star Chow Yun-Fat approaches, Rivers misidentifies his wife as his co-star, Michelle Yeoh, and asks her if she did her own stunts.

Juliette Binoche protests to Rivers that she doesn't want to twirl around and show off her dress, but Rivers says: "Do it for France!"

2000—

Rivers asks Ving Rhames about his chances to win Best Supporting Actor for *The Green Mile*. Only one problem: it's Michael Clarke Duncan, and not Rhames, who is nominated.

1999—

Apparently unfamiliar with television and movie actress Lauren Holly, Rivers looks at her dumbly and barks at Jim Carrey: "Who's your date?"

red-carpet flubs and blunders
by Joan Rivers

Joan asks five-time nominee and one-time winner Robert Duvall if his nomination for *A Civil Action* is the first of his career.

1998—

Rivers greets nominee Peter Fonda, his wife, and his daughter, Bridget Fonda, and tells Bridget that she and "her mother" look so much alike. The woman in question is Bridget's stepmother.

Joan asks Sigourney Weaver the name of the picture for which she's nominated. Weaver is not nominated.

Rivers asks new mom Joan Cusack if she's wearing support undergarments and wonders how long Cusack was in labor.

While interviewing *Amistad* star Djimon Hounsou, Rivers asks if he's written an acceptance speech. Hounsou is not a nominee.

Rivers misidentifies Ben Kingsley as F. Murray Abraham.

1997—

As Emily Watson approaches, Rivers makes fun of her and says, "Nobody knows who the hell she is." But when Watson is within earshot, Rivers gushes, "You were wonderful!"

Rivers asks Barbra Streisand if it's true she wasn't allowed to sleep over at the White House because she's not yet married to boyfriend James Brolin. Streisand tells Rivers her query is "ridiculous."

Rivers, to Jim Carrey: "Are you investing well?"

1996—

Rivers tells the audience that she was at Pat Buchanan's birthday party, where a Nazi jumped out of a cake, and then adds, "[Buchanan's] parents . . . died in the Holocaust . . . they fell off a guard tower."

the
worst
musical
numbers
in Oscar
history

the worst musical numbers in Oscar history

1999—

During the medley of nominations for Best Score, the gruesome and poignant World War II film Saving Private Ryan is among the films subjected to an interpretive dance number.

1988—

An actress playing Snow White sings an off-key rendition of "I Only Have Eyes For You" and tries to hold hands with horrified audience members, including Michelle Pfeiffer and Tom Hanks. Snow White then joins Merv Griffin at a mockup of the Cocoanut Grove, where Merv sings his 1,000-year-old hit, "I've Got a Lovely Bunch of Cocoanuts." Finally, Snow White meets her "blind date," Rob Lowe, who joins her for a deadly version of "Proud Mary," with special updated Oscar-friendly lyrics.

1987—

The show begins with a rendition of "Fugue for Tinhorns," sung by those noted vocalists Telly "Kojak" Savalas, Pat "Happy Days" Morita, and Dom "Maybe They Thought I Was Luciano Pavarotti" DeLuise.

1978—

Debby Boone sings "You Light Up My Life," backed by a chorus of deaf children signing the lyrics. It is later revealed that the children aren't really deaf and didn't know how to sign.

1976—

Live from Amsterdam, a fur-clad Diana Ross takes a ride in a horse-drawn carriage and walks across a bridge while doing a bad job of lip-synching "Theme From Mahogany."

1968—

Wearing a Nehru jacket and Cuban heels and dripping with jewelry, Sammy Davis, Jr., sings "Talk to the Animals" from Dr. Doolittle, adding such Laugh-In–inspired ad libs as "Sock it to me, baby!" and "Here come de judge, here come de judge!"

1959—

The show actually ends 20 minutes EARLY. Host Jerry Lewis waltzes around the stage while the orchestra tries to kill time, and is eventually joined by the likes of Cary Grant and Ingrid Bergman, Natalie Wood, Robert Wagner, Bob Hope, and Zsa Zsa Gabor, all dancing as if they're at a wedding reception. As time drags on and the audience wanders out, many of the couples onstage began to exit as well, leaving Lewis to try such lame schtick as conducting the orchestra like a madman and hitting sour notes on a trumpet. Finally, mercifully, NBC cuts to an instructional film about handguns.

1950—

A whip-cracking Frankie Laine has trouble keeping up with the orchestra as he performs "Mule Train" from the Western Singing Guns. Laine complains to the orchestra leader and also gripes about the lack of snap-crackle-and-pop he gets when he cracks the whip. "Just cover up for me!" he says to the orchestra leader.

20 ways to improve the movie-going experience

20 ways to improve the movie-going experience

a t the ultimate movie theater, these are the rules:

1. All cell phones must be turned off.
2. No pagers.
3. No talking during the movie or during the trailers.
4. No kicking the seat of the person in front of you.
5. No taking off your shoes and putting your smelly feet on the seats in front of you.
6. Anyone violating any of the above policies will be warned once. A second offense will result in immediate ejection from the theater.
7. Bouncers—not skinny, bored, $6-an-hour ushers, but real-life bouncers who look like that Steve guy on "Springer"—will be stationed at theaters to enforce these policies.
8. There will also be a manager on hand, even during the evening and weekend hours, to answer questions and handle complaints from customers.
9. No cashier will ever again be allowed to utter the phrase, "For a quarter more, you can get a larger size." We know we can get a larger size for a quarter more. But if you're offering free refills, what's the point in getting a larger size for a quarter more?

10. There will be a maximum of three trailers before any movie.

11. The trailers will be played at the same volume level as the movie itself.

12. The film will start no later than 10 minutes after the announced starting time.

13. Ten minutes after the movie has started, no one will be allowed to enter the theater.

14. Walls between theaters will be insulated enough so that you don't hear the explosions from "*Die Hard, Die Now, Die Die Die!*" when you're trying to watch "*Silent Pause.*"

15. None of the video games in the lobby will be so loud that you can hear them when you're in the theaters.

16. All films will be projected at optimum light levels. Projectionists will be made to understand that dimming the bulb doesn't extend the life of the bulb—but it does make the film look muddy and dark.

17. Theaters will be air-conditioned, of course—but to a reasonable level. You will not have to bring a parka into the theater in the middle of July.

18. If you insist on bringing a baby to the movies, you must get up and leave THE MOMENT THE BABY STARTS CRYING.

19. Theater employees are not to enter the theater and slouch against the wall for 10 minutes when they should be cleaning the bathrooms or performing some other useful task.

20. If there's a technical problem that lasts for more than five minutes, everybody gets a full refund.

Enjoy the show!

Sources

There are dozens of incredibly useful web sites that I relied upon while writing this book, most notably:

Rotten Tomatoes—www.rottentomatoes.com

Hollywood Bitchslap—www.hollywoodbitchslap.com

Internet Movie Database—www.imdb.com

IFILM, the Internet Movie Guide—www.ifilm.com

OscarWatch—www.oscarwatch.com

The Movie Clichés List—www.moviecliches.com

Mr. Skin—www.mrskin.com

Yahoo! Movies—Greg's Previews—www.upcomingmovies.com

The Smoking Gun—www.thesmokinggun.com

Salon—www.salon.com

I also accessed the web sites of nearly every major entertainment publication and network, from Movieline to *Entertainment Weekly* to MSNBC and CNN, and I conducted countless searches on Lexis-Nexis and Google and used literally hundreds of newspaper and magazine articles to confirm or augment the lists.